SITUATION

BY

JOHNNIE MORTIMER
and
BRIAN COOKE

SAMUEL FRENCH, INC.
45 West 25th Street   NEW YORK 10010
7623 Sunset Boulevard HOLLYWOOD 90046
LONDON   TORONTO

Situation Comedy premiered at the Churchill Theatre in Kent on June 13, 1989. It was produced by Mark Furness and directed by Leon Rubin. Lighting by Richard Caswell and design by Glenn Willoughby. It had the following cast:

CHARLES SUMMERSKILL...Trevor Bannister
ARTHUR GREY ....Brian Murphy
DORIS SUMMERSKILL........... Jane Freeman
BERYL GREY ....Aimi MacDonald
MISS TROTTER................ Pamela Cundell
MAURICE...........................Robert Morris

CHARACTERS

CHARLES SUMMERSKILL
DORIS SUMMERSKILL
ARTHUR GREY
BERYL GREY
MAURICE
MISS TROTTER

SETTING

A West London suburb, such as Barnes.

TIME

The present.

ACT I

Scene 1

*SCENE: There are two playing areas, the Greys'
living room and the Summerskills' living
room, which overlap each other.*

*There is no physical partition, between the Greys'
living room, Stage Right, and the
Summerskills' living room, Stage Left. The
furniture, decor, etc. tell us these are different
rooms in different houses, though, as
specified, they overlap.*

*The Summerskill's living room is in the home of
Charles and Doris Summerskill. It has a
partners' desk, with a chair on either side of it
Downstage Center a metal wastepaper bin
beside it. A telephone on the desk. A dining
table with two upright chairs Downstage Left.
A settee and two armchairs by a coffee table
Upstage Center. A plant next to the settee. A
drinks cabinet against the Upstage Left wall.
An ornamental six-foot screen. A lamp
standard with a large shade. A door leads to
the kitchen Downstage Left. An archway
leads to the hall Upstage Left. We can see the
front door with a window. (This archway is
used for access to the front door, the W.C. and
upstairs.) The furniture suggests a
comfortable income. It is mainly*

reproduction. Everything is spick-and-span. Doris is houseproud and it shows.

The Greys' living room, is in the home of Arthur and Beryl Grey. This has stairs Upstage Right leading up to a half landing, then on, supposedly, to the first floor. A door leads off the half landing to an unseen bathroom. There is a front door Upstage Center with a raised entrance area in front of it, surrounded by bannisters and with one or two steps leading down Upstage Center, a cupboard unit against the bannisters, just Right of steps. An upright piano against the side of the stairs. Downstage Left a dining table with two chairs. Downstage Center a settee and an armchair with a coffee table in front of them. A door leads off to the kitchen Downstage Right with a hatch to the kitchen beside it. A door under the stairs leads to a deep wine cupboard. The furniture is contemporary and quite expensive, but it hasn't been well looked after. The room is noticeably untidy. Beryl is not interested in housework and leaves things where she drops them.

AT RISE: Summerskills living room, desk area. The effect is a pool of LIGHT around the desk area.

Early evening in late summer. CHARLES SUMMERSKILL paces up and down, deep in thought. HE is a sharp dresser, rather extrovert in style. At the moment HE is in shirtsleeves and a fancy waistcoat. HE speaks with a public school accent, though both his clothes and his mind are more vulgar than this might suggest.

ARTHUR GREY *is standing on the desk. HE is also seeking inspiration, making little noises of concentration. His clothes are casual and not well looked after. A cardigan and rumpled grey flannel trousers with a shirt that needs pressing. ARTHUR has left behind a northern working-class background, but traces of it still show in his speech.*

ARTHUR. If we can't think of a plot, let's at least think of a title. It might start us off ... something sensible and believable.

(*A long moment as THEY cudgel their brains, long enough for us to fix this position in our minds. Eventually CHARLES snaps his fingers. HE's got it ...*)

CHARLES. "I ... Married ... A ... Mermaid!"
ARTHUR. I can see several problems there ...
CHARLES. Really? I can only see one. Think of it ... a dumb, blonde mermaid. Thirty-eight, twenty-two ... one pound forty a pound ...
ARTHUR. (*Climbs down from desk.*) Is it different enough?

CHARLES. No. Needs a gimmick ... "I Married An *Invisible* Mermaid!"

ARTHUR. Can't we try, just once, to write a script with some subtlety and sophistication?

CHARLES. (*Rummages amongst some papers on the desk.*) How about ... (*Finds notes.*) "Mr. Bloody's Knicker Factory!"

ARTHUR. Oh God, not again.

CHARLES. (*Reading notes, enthusiastic.*) Mr. Bloody ... that's his name, so they can't touch us for it ... crusty, but lovable ... owns a knicker factory in Wigan. Dumb blonde secretary ... (*Makes boobs gesture.*) .. with big ambitions. Eager, but accident prone young assistant ...

ARTHUR. Charles, you've got to stop this lone crusade to bring quality to television.

CHARLES. Or ... (*Rummages.*) There's "Gumshoe Granny!" A crusty, but lovable geriatric, fighting crime in Wigan ...

ARTHUR. Why Wigan?

(*Gradually bring up LIGHTS on the two main sets.*)

CHARLES. Third rule of comedy. "Wigan is funny." Opening episode ... her knickers are stolen by the arch-criminal, Mr. Bloody ...

(*During the above, ARTHUR flicks his lighter, sets fire to the sheet of paper CHARLES is reading from.*)

CHARLES. ... Uh! (*Drops smouldering paper into metal wastebin.*) You're not besotted, then?

(*ARTHUR shakes his head.*)

CHARLES. All right ... think of another title...

(*The kitchen door opens and DORIS, Charles' wife, enters. SHE wears a flowered pinafore over her matronly figure.*)

DONNA. Next door's cat's done a whoopsie in the bird bath.

(*ARTHUR and CHARLES look at each other hopefully.*)

CHARLES. No, it's too long.
DORIS. (*To Charles.*) Dinner in twenty minutes, dear. (*To Arthur.*) Are you staying, Arthur?
ARTHUR. No, no. Beryl will be cooking mine ... I'm afraid.

(*ARTHUR, gathering his notes together, has a thought, prompted by the notes. DORIS exits to the kitchen.*)

ARTHUR. I still think there's something in a situation comedy about two writers, writing a ... a...

CHARLES. Situation comedy?

ARTHUR. Yes!

(*The TELEPHONE RINGS. CHARLES crosses to answer it.*)

CHARLES. It might work. If we set it in Wigan ... and one of them married a mermaid ... (*To phone.*) Hullo? (*Listens, stunned.*) What? Yes, he's here, madam, but ... What? The father of your child? Oh, I'm sure you've made a mist ... photographs? This sounds remarkably like blackmail, young woman!

ARTHUR. (*Worried.*) Wha' ... who ... ?

CHARLES. (*Waving him away.*) Send them to the newspapers, see if he cares! Yes! We're calling your bluff!

ARTHUR. (*Snatching the phone.*) Give me that! (*To phone.*) Hullo?

CHARLES. (*Smug.*) It's our agent.

ARTHUR. (*Sighs. To phone.*) Hullo, Maurice. No, no. It's his usual six o'clock nervous breakdown ...

CHARLES. Six o'clock! (*Checks watch, crosses and pours himself a stiff whisky.*) En garde, liver!

ARTHUR. (*To phone.*)Yes ... Yes ... No ... we haven't come up with an idea ...

CHARLES. "Mr. Bloody's Knicker Factory!"

ARTHUR. (*To phone.*) Not a single one, no. We've only been back a week. (*Continues to respond during the following.*)

DORIS. (*Bustles in from the kitchen.*) Are you two still at it? Oh ... who's on the phone?

CHARLES. (*Refilling his drink.*) It's Arthur.

DORIS. The *other* end.

CHARLES. Oh, some poor girl he's got into trouble. It seems she's blackmailing him.

DORIS. (*Not really listening.*) Oh, that's nice. (*SHE exits to kitchen again.*)

CHARLES. (*Looking after her.*) It's in one ear and out of the other. With an echo.

ARTHUR. (*Covering phone.*) He wants to drop 'round to see us, tonight ... okay?

CHARLES. Out of the question! Bloodsucking vampire!

ARTHUR. (*To phone.*) Charles says he looks forward to seeing you ... About eightish, yes.

CHARLES. He's cutting it a bit fine. He has to be back in his coffin by midnight.

ARTHUR. Yes, I'll be there, too, Maurice. 'Bye ... bye ... (*Phone down, bitter.*) He's going to New York. Tony's got *another* play opening. On Broadway.

CHARLES. Well, naturally. It's Thursday.

ARTHUR. That's four. Four plays! All successful! Winning awards! What can *we* set against that?

CHARLES. We've got an award ... (*Indicates a small trophy on a shelf.*)

ARTHUR. One! (*Reads the inscription.*) "Best T.V. Comedy Part for a Budgie. 1973!" Presented by Spillikins Sand Sheets! Hah! (*A thought.*) Incidentally, you've had this for six months, it's my turn. (*HE keeps hold of it and takes it with him when he exits.*)

CHARLES. Take it ... (*Pours himself another drink.*)

ARTHUR. (*Checks watch.*) I'm going home. Beryl's cooking her speciality tonight ... swill.

(*HE puts on his jacket, as DORIS comes from the kitchen carrying a steaming casserole dish, etc. SHE's wearing oven gloves.*)

DORIS. Oh, you're off then, Arthur?

ARTHUR. Yes ... (*Sniffs.*) Oh ... ooh ... Oh that looks good. It's ... erm ... it's ... No, don't tell me. I've seen it before ... along time ago. Food! That's it!

DORIS. It's only steak and kidney pie, with crusty pastry and tiny new potatoes and minted peas ...

ARTHUR. (*Groans.*) Oh ...

CHARLES. Don't dribble over my dinner!

ARTHUR. I'm going. We'll see you later. (*Exits.*)

DORIS. (*Calls after him.*) Oh, don't forget the slides! (*Sound of front DOOR CLOSING.*)

CHARLES. Shh! I've spent the entire day *not* reminding him ...

DORIS. Best part of the holiday, watching the slides. They're fun.

CHARLES. Fun?!

DORIS. Well, I think it's ... (*A thought. SHE indicates the telephone.*) How d'you mean ... "Blackmailing him?"

CHARLES. (*Sighs.*) Let it go, Doris. Let it go. (*HE follows her into the kitchen.*)

(*LIGHTS fade and rise on: Greys' living room. A couple of hours later, night. ARTHUR comes down the stairs, buttoning up a fresh shirt.*)

ARTHUR. (*Calls.*) Beryl ... we're going to be late.

(*BERYL enters from the kitchen, cigarette in mouth. She's slightly flashy in her dress, but sexy with it. She's a little younger than Arthur.*)

BERYL. All right, all right. I'm just setting the table. (*SHE tosses a knife and fork onto the table.*) There. (*Exits to the kitchen, again.*)

ARTHUR. Don't go to any trouble ... (*HE crosses to the sideboard, takes out several boxes of holiday slides, a small slide projector and a folded screen. HE takes a few slides from the box, holds them up to the light.*) World premiere at the

Summerskills' tonight. Mmm ... D' you know, I should have had a flash in that Spanish nightclub.

(*BERYL has entered, carrying a plate containing a lumpy stew. SHE drops it on the table.*)

BERYL. Mm. Might have livened things up a bit.

ARTHUR. Trouble was, I'd left it behind in my other trousers. (*Sits at table.*)

BERYL. Really? (*Gives him a look.*) Eat your dinner. (*SHE sits beside him and continues painting her nails.*)

ARTHUR. Y'see, when the light is ... (*Looks at food.*) Ah. Yes. What *is* this, Beryl?

BERYL. What's it look like?

ARTHUR. Pedigree Chum.

BERYL. Well, it isn't. It's Boil-In-The-Bag Beef Bourgignon.

ARTHUR. Ah ... (*Tastes it, chews.*) I think I'd prefer Pedigree Chum.

BERYL. (*Indicating slides.*) How many of 'em turned out?

ARTHUR. Every single one.

BERYL. Oh joy ...

ARTHUR. Three hundred and sixty. (*Chews with distaste.*) Aren't you ... er ... aren't you having any of this muck?

BERYL. What's wrong with it?

ARTHUR. Nothing. I mean ... it's very ... Perhaps if it was warm? Oh, there's a bit of the bag here. That's quite tasty.

BERYL. You've a sharp tongue on you, Arthur.

ARTHUR. You need one with this stuff. (*Stands.*) I think I'll give the waste disposal an ulcer.

BERYL. You don't want any afters, do you?

ARTHUR. No! No, I'll make do with the usual indigestion tablets. (*Exits to kitchen with his plate, etc. as the FRONT-BELL RINGS.*)

BERYL. (*Crosses to answer it, calling back towards the kitchen.*) We've run out again. You go through them like sweets. (*Opens the front door.*)

(*A small bird-like woman in an apron works her way in. This is MISS TROTTER, a spinster neighbor. SHE is in her late forties/early fifties.*)

MISS TROTTER. Now, I can't stay ...

BERYL. Oh, good.

MISS TROTTER. I just popped 'round to borrow a cup of sugar. (*All in one breath.*) Have you heard about the Newton's boy? Got the girl from Tescos in trouble ... the one from the cash desk ...

BERYL. Brown or white?

MISS TROTTER. Oh, they're all the same to him. The bank manager ... he's been seen near Mrs. Wilson's clothes-line again ... that's the seventh pair she's lost ...

(*ARTHUR enters from the kitchen, sees her, does an abrupt about turn, but it's too late.*)

MISS TROTTER. Oh, hullo, Mr. Grey!
ARTHUR. Ah ... hullo, Miss Trotter. How are you?

(*BERYL exits to kitchen.*)

MISS TROTTER. I'm my usual self.
ARTHUR. I'm sorry to hear it.
MISS TROTTER. But the vicar, he's got his old trouble back. They may have to remove it completely. Of course, you'll have missed all this, being abroad with your friends. You won't have heard about Mrs. Pettifer's knee ...
ARTHUR. Oh, it was headlines in all the Spanish newspapers.
MISS TROTTER. Really? You should have put all this in one of your little television shows. I'd write it myself, but I've so much to do.
ARTHUR. Yes, it would involve leaving the window.
MISS TROTTER. I mean, take that Mr. Larkin ... always down the netball courts with his binoculars. Studying birds, he calls it, but I ...

(*BERYL returns and hands her a cup of sugar.*)

MISS TROTTER. What's this?
BERYL. Sugar.
MISS TROTTER. Oh, yes. Thank you. What was I about to say ... ?
ARTHUR. (*Easing her towards the front door.*) Goodbye.
MISS TROTTER. Oh, was that it? Yes ... goodbye. (*SHE exits.*)
ARTHUR. (*Closes the front door.*) Phew ...
BERYL. Fastest gums in the West.
ARTHUR. Oh, she means well ... in her own evil way. (*Looks at his watch.*) We'd better go. Bring the slides, Beryl.

(*SHE reluctantly picks up some of the boxes of slides, but deliberately leaves a few. ARTHUR crosses to a door under the stairs. HE opens the door. Exits for a moment, then brings some bottles of wine with hand written labels.*)

ARTHUR. Now ... I promised I'd take some bottles of my homemade wine.
BERYL. Thrill.
ARTHUR. Either that, or I promised I wouldn't. I know they were very enthusiastic. But which one? The full-bodied nettle, or the rhubarb nouveau?

BERYL. They all strip the enamel off your teeth.

ARTHUR. You know your trouble? You haven't got a palate.

BERYL. I had before I drank that stuff! D'you really have to take it?

ARTHUR. Certainly. I don't want to disappoint them, do I?

(THEY exit through their front door. LIGHTS cross-fade and rise on Summerskills' living room.

Dinner is over. CHARLES enters from the kitchen, carrying an ice bucket. DORIS close behind, still wearing her pinafore.)

CHARLES. I hope he doesn't bring any of his Chateau Gnatspiss with him.

DORIS. Language.

CHARLES. Still, the stomach's lined. (*Pours himself a Scotch.*) You do a marvellous snake and pigmy pie. If you were as good in bed as you are in the kitchen, I'd marry you. (*Gives her a sexy squeeze.*)

DORIS. We are married.

CHARLES. Yes. That was a joke, Doris.

DORIS. (*Genuine.*) Oh. You should tell me when you're making a joke. I could laugh.

CHARLES. No, I want you to really enjoy it. Not *pretend*.

DORIS. What's wrong with me in bed, anyway?

CHARLES. Same thing.

(*The DOORBELL CHIMES.*)

DORIS. Oops! Don't let them in 'til I've got my pinny off!

CHARLES. (*Bounds to front door.*) Roll up! Roll up! See Doris in her pinny!

DORIS. Ooh ... ! (*Hastily exits to kitchen.*)

(*CHARLES opens the front door to admit Arthur and Beryl. ARTHUR carries the projector, a rolled up screen and some bottles of home-made wine. BERYL carries the boxes of slides.*)

CHARLES. Be quick! Oh ... tch! ... you've just missed her.

ARTHUR. Who?

CHARLES. Doris. Stark naked, except for the jackboots.

BERYL. Oh, fun and games.

CHARLES. Come in, come in. (*Gives Beryl a kiss on the cheek.*) Hullo, Beryl, darling. Let me take your coat ... and your dress ... and your underwear ...

(*BERYL giggles. CHARLES amuses her almost as much as he does himself.*)

BERYL. They wouldn't suit you, Charlie.

CHARLES. Oohoo ... (*Hangs her coat up.*)

ARTHUR. I've brought some bottles of my wine.

CHARLES. Ah, I was afraid you might ... uh ... have forgotten. It's not the rhubarb again, is it?

ARTHUR. No, no ... (*Hands over bottles.*) It's pea.

CHARLES. Oh, yes?

ARTHUR. And I don't want any remarks, I've heard them all. Just pour out while I set everything up.

(*CHARLES pours four glasses of wine, looking dubious. ARTHUR sets up the screen, loads the slides into the projector, etc. BERYL sits on the settee. During the rest of the scene, their glasses are kept topped up with either whisky or wine.*)

ARTHUR. The whole holiday is here ...

BERYL. (*To Charles.*) It's going to be a long evening.

(*DORIS comes out from the kitchen without her pinny.*)

BERYL. Hullo, Doris. You got dressed, then?

DORIS. Oh, yes. What?

CHARLES. (*Hands her a glass of wine.*) Have a drop of homemade.

DORIS. Oh, lovely. Hullo, Beryl. (*Looks at wine glass.*) What is it this time?

CHARLES. Well, according to him ...

ARTHUR. Ah! Let her taste it first.

DORIS. It's a lovely color. (*Sips.*) Mmm ... it tastes like ... it tastes like ...

CHARLES. Pea?

DORIS. Oh, no, no. It's very nice ... whatever it is. (*Sits.*)

ARTHUR. (*Moves away from the screen, it slowly collapses. HE notices.*) Wait! (*HE re-erects the screen and walks towards the projector. The screen collapses again.*) Now then, the first slide ... Oh, damn! (*HE fiddles with the screen, realizes it won't stay up.*) Oh, no ... the spring's gone!

CHARLES. Oh, dear, oh, dear!

ARTHUR. It's useless!

CHARLES. Oh, what a shame! I was really looking forward to those slides. Disappointing ... very disappointing ... (*Cheerful.*) Still ...

ARTHUR. I'll use the wall ... (*Gestures towards the audience.*)

CHARLES. (*Dismay.*) The wall ...?

ARTHUR. I'll project them on the wall!

DORIS. It won't mark it, will it?

ARTHUR. No. Might be even better. I can blow them up, y'see ...

BERYL. Best suggestion I've heard all night.

ARTHUR. (*Starts projector.*) Oh, yes, there we are ...

ARTHUR. "Beryl packing my pyjamas."

CHARLES. (*Nudges Beryl.*) Oohoo! Straight into the hardcore!

ARTHUR. I shot this one at F8 and a hundred and twenty-fifth of a second. The lighting isn't what I would have liked, though I did bounce a five hundred watt reflector off the ceiling to provide that rather effective back-lighting ...

(*During this, BERYL and CHARLES yawn and cross their legs simultaneously. DORIS is fascinated.*)

ARTHUR. ... and on to the next one.

CHARLES. There's more?!

BERYL. He's got three hundred and sixty of 'em.

CHARLES. (*Dismayed.*) That's nice.

(*During the following, CHARLES sips his wine and reacts with distaste. Tips it into a handy plant pot. Surreptitiously reaches for the whisky bottle and pours himself a Scotch. BERYL nudges him, gives him her glass. HE does the same with hers. ARTHUR continues to project his slides, enthusiastic.*)

ARTHUR. The same scene, shot from another angle. I used a filter on this one ...

DORIS. Oh, I use them for making coffee.

ARTHUR. (*Uncertain.*) Yes ... very good. Now ... ah! Closing the suitcase ... (*Click.*) In the hall ... And at last we reach ...

CHARLES. Spain!

ARTHUR. (*Click.*) ... the front doorstep.

BERYL. Arthur ... !

ARTHUR. (*Flustered.*) Yes. I'll ... er ... I'll move on a bit ... (*HE skips through several slides.*) Spain!

DORIS. Lovely.

ARTHUR. Here we are at the hotel ... "Beryl *un*packing my pyjamas."

(*CHARLES and BERYL sigh in despair. The front DOORBELL RINGS.*)

CHARLES. Doorbell, Doris. I can't go. My legs have gone to sleep ... and who can blame them?

(*BERYL laughs. DORIS crosses to the front door.*)

ARTHUR. Don't worry, your favorite person comes on in a minute.

CHARLES. Do I, really? Press on!

DORIS. (*Opens front door to admit MAURICE, their literary agent.*) Oh, do come in. (*Calls.*) It's Maurice!

(*MAURICE is slightly younger than they are. HE's very much a man of the theatre and something of a snob. Well dressed, his camel hair overcoat around his shoulders. HE breezes in confidently. HE carries a document case. DORIS puts the main light on.*)

MAURICE. Hullo, boys. Don't get up.
ARTHUR. Maurice. Glass of wine?
MAURICE. Is it that filthy muck you make yourself?
ARTHUR. Yes.
MAURICE. I'll force myself.

(*ARTHUR pours him a glass.*)

MAURICE. Evening, ladies ...
BERYL. Maurice.
MAURICE. Well, that's enough lower middle-class social chit-chat. To business ... (*Sits.*) Does the thirty-first of this month mean anything to you boys?

(*A moment's hesitation as CHARLES and ARTHUR look at each other.*)

CHARLES. Er ... (*Sings.*) Happy birthday to you ...
ARTHUR. (*Joining in.*) ... birthday to you ...

MAURICE. No, no, no. It's the date you are supposed to deliver yet another of your riotous half hours of high jinks for the unwashed. "Anything can happen when Mabel burns the joint and Fred's boss is coming to dinner" sort of thing.

ARTHUR. (*Annoyed.*) You've got no respect for our work, have you?! (*Hands him a glass of wine.*)

BERYL. Oh, gawd. Here we go again.

MAURICE. Of course I have. It's quite good ... of its type. (*Sips, reacts.*) Nggh ... So I'm told.

ARTHUR. See! See!

BERYL. (*To Doris.*) If they're going to talk shop, let's go in the kitchen and do something more exciting.

DORIS. Well, there's the washing up.

BERYL. That'll do. You wash and I'll watch.

(*THEY exit to kitchen. BERYL takes the whiskey bottle with her as an afterthought.*)

CHARLES. Maurice, it's difficult to set up a new series. We do have one idea ...

ARTHUR. That we've dismissed!

CHARLES. That we've dismissed ... so we haven't got anything, come to think of it. Still, it's better than nothing.

MAURICE. Well, keep at it. You've always come up with something. That last series of yours ... er ... er ... Very popular. Ran for years.

ARTHUR. (*A trap.*) What was it called, Maurice?

MAURICE. (*Doesn't know.*) Uh ... your last series? Hahaha ... as if I wouldn't remember the title? (*Looks at his watch.*) I can't stay long. I'm on my way to the airport ...

CHARLES. A white, divorced, father of three marries a black, divorced mother of two ...

MAURICE. I *like* it! I thought you said you had no ideas?

ARTHUR. That *was* the last series! (*To Charles.*) He never even watched it!

MAURICE. I most certainly did!

ARTHUR. You never mentioned it.

MAURICE. I was being tactful. I was afraid you might ask me what I thought of it.

ARTHUR. What *did* you think of it?

MAURICE. (*Defiant.*) Very popular! (*Another swig of wine. Shudders.*) Nggh!

CHARLES. Another one?

MAURICE. Thank you.

CHARLES. Masochist. (*Fills his glass again.*) You're off to New York?

MAURICE. Yes. Tony's opening night. And, of course, he's been nominated for the theatrical awards. The ... uh ... Tony's.

ARTHUR. They've even named the bloody award after him!

MAURICE. Yes, well, I ... er ... (*Swigs wine.*) Nggh ... I'll be back in a week. I expect you'll have a script, brimming with chuckles and wheezes ...

ARTHUR. "Chuckles and wheezes?!" Haven't you forgotten custard pies ... and ... and dropping trousers ... and knickers and Wigan...?

MAURICE. That's the way! Get it down on paper ... (*A last swig as HE heads for the front door, escorted by CHARLES.*) Nggh ... Thank you for the wine, it was vile. (*Exits.*)

CHARLES. (*Calling after him.*) 'Bye, Maurice. Watch out for silver bullets. (*Closes front door.*) There is nothing worse than having your agent come 'round and nag you in your own home.

ARTHUR. Let's get back to the slides.

CHARLES. I tell a lie. There is one thing worse. Just a second, I need something first ... (*Lurches across to the drinks, as Quasimodo.*) The Bells! The Bells!

(*Pours himself a stiff glass of Bells whisky from a new bottle. During the following, the LADIES return. BERYL brings her own whisky bottle, now noticeably emptier.*)

ARTHUR. Look, if you don't want to watch them, you've only got to say so.

CHARLES. Do you really mean that?

ARTHUR. (*Hesitates.*) No, I don't. Sit down.

DORIS. Oh, has Maurice gone, then?

CHARLES. Yes. Flying to New York. Last seen as the outline of a bat against the full moon.

ARTHUR. The slides ... sit down. Where were we up to?

BERYL. The interval ... (*To Charles.*) I'll have a whisky on a stick, please.

(*CHARLES refills her glass and THEY resume their earlier positions. THEY are beginning to feel the effect of the drink. ARTHUR turns the main LIGHT OFF. Starts to project the slides.*)

ARTHUR. Now then ... I could go back to the beginning?

CHARLES. No!

BERYL. No! Look, Arthur, can't you skip the boring bits?

ARTHUR. What, *all* of them?

BERYL. Just get on with it.

ARTHUR. Right ... (*Click.*) Ah, now there's Doris on the beach, with a donkey.

CHARLES. (*To Beryl.*) Doris is on the left.

(*BERYL laughs.*)

CHARLES. No, I tell a lie ...

ARTHUR. (*Click.*) There's me and Beryl sunbathing.

CHARLES. You look incredibly sexy in that wet bathing suit.

ARTHUR. Thank you. (*Click.*) Doris again. Asleep on the beach.

DORIS. Who put that apple in my mouth?

CHARLES. Hehe ...

ARTHUR. (*Click.*) Now, here's all four of us. I had a delayed exposure there.

BERYL. (*Nudges Charles.*) Nudge, nudge, wink, wink.

(*A final click. The end of the rack.*)

ARTHUR. And that's the end ...

CHARLES. Oh, good.

ARTHUR. Of the first box.

CHARLES. Oh, God.

(*ARTHUR puts the main LIGHT on and starts to sort through the other boxes of slides. CHARLES and BERYL light cigarettes.*)

DORIS. Oh, it was a lovely holiday. All that sun and seashine ... ooops. That wine of yours has got my tang all tonguled up ... ooh.

CHARLES. You've had enough, Doris. (*Squints at her.*) You're starting to look attractive. (*Pours Scotch in Beryl's glass.*) Say when ...

BERYL. Anytime you're in the mood.

CHARLES. Oohoo. One of these days I might take you up on that.

ARTHUR. Beryl, you didn't bring box number two!

BERYL. Well, skip it. Get on to that one where Charles stuffed the crab down your swim trunks.

ARTHUR. I can't show them out of order. Tech ... It won't take me a minute to pop home and get it.

DORIS. (*Fans air.*) I'll come with you. I could do with a fresh of breath air ... (*Stands.*)

ARTHUR. Shall I bring another bottle of the ... er ... ?

CHARLES. No, no, no, no. Have pity.

ARTHUR. Right. After you, Doris. You can't show them out of order!

(*HE and DORIS exit through the front door.*)

CHARLES. Absolutely. (*Instantly randy. To Beryl.*) Now what's it to be? Five minutes of passionate ecstasy, or another Scotch?

BERYL. (*Giggles.*) I'll have some soda with it this time.

CHARLES. Spurned again. (*Pours another drink, looks around.*) Soda?

BERYL. Trouble with you, Charles, you give up too easily.

CHARLES. You mean, there's a sporting chance of a spot of nookie, at last?

BERYL. Don't be silly. I'm a married woman.

CHARLES. I give up. Soda ... (*Exits to kitchen.*)

BERYL. See what I mean? (*SHE follows him.*)

(*LIGHTS cross-fade and up on Greys' living room. ARTHUR and DORIS in through the front door. His coat is pulled up over their heads. It's obviously raining outside.*)

ARTHUR. Oh, dear, dear, dear. That came on sudden.

DORIS. I should have brought my mac.

ARTHUR. Oh, you can pop back for it when the rain stops. Come in. Now then, box two ... (*Finds the left-behind boxes.*) Ah! Sit down for a minute ... There's some good shots in here. Plants and things ... There's one of two cactuses ... uh ... two cactieye ...

DORIS. One cactus next to another cactus? (*SHE starts to tidy up, automatically. Emptying ashtrays, etc.*)

ARTHUR. Yes. Thank you. (*Indicates his racks of homemade wine.*) I wonder if you can make wine from cactuses?

DORIS. (*Arch.*) It might taste a bit ... sharp.

ARTHUR. I suppose it ... (*Sees her little joke.*) Oh ... ohoho ... very good! (*Takes a bottle from the cupboard.*) Ah, this is rather special. A full bodied radish. Try a drop. (*Unscrews the top. Pours two glasses.*)

DORIS. Oh, I shouldn't. I'll have ankles like balloons tomorrow.

ARTHUR. Sit down, Doris. No point in doing that. Beryl's due to tidy the place up in a couple of weeks, anyway.

DORIS. (*Sits.*) Sorry ... habit.

ARTHUR. Just try this ... (*Gives her glass of wine.*) Radish. It's three years old.

DORIS. Oh ... (*To glass.*) Happy birthday! (*Giggles.*) Hehe ... hoohoo.

(*SHE drinks it back in one long swig. ARTHUR does the full wine bit, holding it up to the light, sniffing and swirling, then he sips it.*)

ARTHUR. Mmm ... mmm ... just a hint ... of flint. I suggest you sip it slowly and ... (*See she's holding out her empty glass.*) Oh.

DORIS. I'll have a repeat. Hic!

ARTHUR. No. Better yet, I've a carrot in the wine cellar.

(*HE opens the door under the stairs, exits. SHE follows him.*)

DORIS. Oh ...

(*LIGHTS cross-fade and up on Summerskill's living room. Some time later. CHARLES enters from the kitchen, crosses to a window and peers out. BERYL follows him. THEY'VE both had a few drinks and are still drinking.*)

CHARLES. Still raining.

BERYL. Is it? (*Holds out her hand.*) I can't feel it.

CHARLES. They won't come back in this. (*Helps himself to another drink.*) Time for another little drinkie-poo.

BERYL. You've had enough, Charlie. You're looking very blurred.

CHARLES. No, no, no. Watch me walk a straight line ... (*Walks carefully but erratically towards the settee, weaving all over the place; sits beside her.*) There!

BERYL. (*Impressed.*) Very good!

CHARLES. No, I always know when I've had too much to drink. I get maudlin. (*Instantly gets maudlin, lays his head on Beryl's shoulder.*) Doris doesn't understand me, you know.

BERYL. There, there, there.

CHARLES. She's not as keen on the ... physical side of things as I am.

BERYL. How d'you mean?

CHARLES. You know ... the physical side.

BERYL. What, like jogging?

CHARLES. (*Decides this word will do as well as any.*) Yes ... jogging. I mean, she will jog ... every so often but she's not enthusiastic about it.

BERYL. Can't you, you know, do it on your own?

CHARLES. Of course you can't.

BERYL. But I've seen fellers doing it ... down the High Street ... on their own.

CHARLES. Beryl, what are you talking about?

BERYL. Jogging. What are you talking about?

CHARLES. I was ... I was employing the word as a ... euphemism for ... for ... how's your father

BERYL. He's been dead ten years.

CHARLES. Who has?

BERYL. My father. Heart attack. I think it was the jogging.

CHARLES. Can we start again, Beryl? I was referring to ... and let's not beat about the bush ... what-ho!

BERYL. Oh, you mean sex!

CHARLES. You could call it that, I suppose.

BERYL. And Doris isn't keen?

CHARLES. She jots downs recipes in the middle of it! Oh ...

BERYL. There, there, there.

CHARLES. And another thing ... she doesn't laugh at my jokes.

BERYL. You ... tell her jokes while you're actually ...?

CHARLES. No, no, no. Generally ... all the time. They're too subtle for her ... but you laugh at them.

BERYL. Like the time you put the rubber lizard in Arthur's soup!

(*THEY both laugh at the memory. HE tops her glass up.*)

BERYL. Ta! I think I need to powder my nose.

CHARLES. Well, you know where it is. First on the left.

BERYL. Which is left?

CHARLES. I'll show you ... (*HE leads her into the hall, out of our sight.*)

(*LIGHTS cross-fade and up on Greys' living room. Some time later. DORIS comes from the wine cellar. ARTHUR close behind, SHE is carrying her glass. ARTHUR is opening another bottle of wine. THEY'RE both tiddly.*)

DORIS. Very nice ... strong. Did you say it was a claret.

ARTHUR. No, no ... a carrot. And do try this one. It's a rather presumptuous sultana ... (*Fills another two glasses.*)

DORIS. Just a small one. We ought to be getting back, they'll be worried. Well, Beryl will...

ARTHUR. So will Charles.

DORIS. No, he won't. He never even notices when I'm not there.

ARTHUR. How do you know?

DORIS. What?

ARTHUR. How do you know he doesn't notice that you're not there? When you're not there. To notice.

DORIS. (*Finds this funny. Laughs.*) Hoohoo ... (*Suddenly upset.*) He says I'm fat!

ARTHUR. Oh, no, no. Never. I mean, you're not ... thin. But you're certainly not ... You're pleasantly ... Rubensesques. Or ... or ... well fleshed, is a phrase I ...

DORIS. You're working your way back to fat! (*Swigs her wine.*) He also says I've got no sense of humor and I'm no good in bed!

ARTHUR. (*A beat.*) But never fat!

DORIS. I'm sorry. Don't mind me. It's the carrot talking.

ARTHUR. He doesn't appreciate you, d'you know that? I mean, your dumplings are a work of art. If ... if Beethoven had made dumplings instead of writing symphonies, we'd... we'd ...

DORIS. Probably never have heard of him.

ARTHUR. No ... I mean, yes.

DORIS. Doesn't exactly sound the same, does it? Beethoven's Unfinished Dumpling. (*Laughs.*)

ARTHUR. Especially since it was Schubert. No, what I'm saying is ... is that Beryl, though she isn't fat and is good in b ... but she can't cook! She burns salad. And she' s not exactly houseproud. (*Indicates 'round.*) The dustiest thing in the whole place is the vacuum cleaner. Have some more sultana ...

DORIS. Ooh, I don't think I ... Oooops. (*SHE spills some wine on her dress.*)

ARTHUR. Oh, dear. Would you like a tea towel?

DORIS. No, no. I couldn't drink another thing. (*Stands.*) We really should be getting back ... Ooh, I'm quite squiffy. I must pull myself together. (*Appears to do so.*) That's better. (*SHE slumps again.*)

ARTHUR. I'll get your coat ...

(*DORIS suddenly falls back over the arm of the settee, legs flying.*)

ARTHUR. D-Doris? Doris!

(*Goes to BLACK, so that both sets are now in darkness.*)

Scene 2

SCENE: Summerskill's living room.

AT RISE: The following morning. Bring up LIGHTS. CHARLES is asleep on the settee, his head on a pile of cushions. HE's covered with a colorful blanket/travel rug. The glasses and bottles of the previous night are in evidence. A morning newspaper comes through the letterbox, making a clatter. It wakes him. HE sits up. HE's wearing a vest and underpants. HE has a hangover.

CHARLES. Ooo ... unf ... ooh ... my head! Aspirins ... (*Calls towards stairs.*) Doris! Where are the aspirins? Doris ...! (*HE becomes aware of a body under the blanket next to him. HE feels it cautiously.*) Doris?

(*The lump sits up. It's BERYL. SHE's wearing a slip.*)

BERYL. Morning, Charlie.

CHARLES. Oh ... my ... God! (*HE leaps from the settee, clutching a cushion for modesty.*)

BERYL. (*Stretches and yawns, unabashed.*) Ooh, I'm thoroughly ashamed of myself. I really am. (*SHE isn't.*)

CHARLES. (*During the following, CHARLES finds his trousers and struggles into them.*) What ... what ... you ... Beryl, what have we done?!

BERYL. I'll give you three guesses.

CHARLES. I don't mean *that!* I meant ... good grief ... You should have stopped me! All you had to say was "No!"

BERYL. That was the word! I couldn't remember it. (*Lights a cigarette.*)

CHARLES. It was the drink. Ooh ... (*Holds head.*) You should never mix the grain and the pea.

BERYL. Oh, c'mon, Charlie. You've been trying to talk me into it for years.

CHARLES. Yes, but you know me ... that's just my way of saying "hullo."

BERYL. (*Sexy.*) Hullo!

CHARLES. Stop th ... Beryl! Tchee ... Oh, Lord. I ... (*Suddenly curious.*) How was I?

BERYL. You're a pistol.

CHARLES. Really? Well, I ... (*Alarm.*) What about Arthur?!

BERYL. He's a popgun.

CHARLES. No! What'll he *say*? We've been friends for years. This may affect it. (*HE paces.*)

BERYL. It's possible.

CHARLES. Nothing happened! That's it! It was completely innocent! You passed out on the settee ... and ... and I covered you with a blanket and slept upstairs! I didn't touch you once ...

BERYL. Twice.

CHARLES. What?

BERYL. You didn't touch me twice.

CHARLES. (*Remembering.*) Oh, yes ... No! Look, get dressed before Doris ... Where *is* Doris? (*Looks around fearfully.*)

BERYL. When last seen, she was with Arthur.

CHARLES. Yes, of course ... (*Thinks it through.*) Arthur? (*HE dials the phone.*)

(*Greys' living room. The room is empty. Bottles and glasses still there. The bathroom door on the half landing is ajar. We hear a SHOWER RUNNING and an occasional "la-la-ing" from a MUFFLED FEMALE VOICE. Phone starts to RING. A beat, then ARTHUR comes*

*down the stairs from the bedroom. HE is
pulling on his wooly dressing gown over his
pyjamas. HE's got one sock on. HE has a bad
hangover.*)

ARTHUR. Ooh ... hang on, hang on ... Ooh.
(*Picks up phone.*) Oooh!
CHARLES. (*To Beryl.*) Well, he's there. (*To
phone.*) Hullo, Arthur?
ARTHUR. Ooh ... hullo, Charles. (*HE hangs
up, groans and sinks into a chair.*) Ooh ...
CHARLES. Hullo? Damn ... (*Redials.*) He's
hung up!
BERYL. That's typical Arthur. He's not at his
best in the morning. Or any other time of the day.
ARTHUR. (*Jerks awake as the phone RINGS
again.*) Hullo?
CHARLES. Arthur ... it's Doris ...
ARTHUR. Hullo, Doris.
CHARLES. No, no. Don't hang up! I'm
wondering if you've got any idea where she is?
ARTHUR. Erm ... ooh, I ... I don't ... don't
remember much about last night. I'll ask Beryl. I
can hear her in the shower ...

(*During the above, the la-la-ing" from the
bathroom has got a little louder.*)

ARTHUR. (*HE lays the phone aside.*) Oooh ...
(*Weaves towards the bathroom.*)

CHARLES. (*Baffled, to Beryl.*) He's gone to ask you.

(*ARTHUR has reached the bathroom door. HE goes inside.*)

ARTHUR. Beryl, have you got any idea where ... (*Comes out like a shot from a gun, flustered and babbling back into the bathroom.*) Oh, I do beg your pardon! I ... I must get that lock fixed ... I ... ooh ... I didn't see anything at all! (*Picks up the phone.*) No, I'm sorry. It wasn't Beryl, it was ... (*Realization.*) Doris?! (*Slams phone down, stricken.*)

CHARLES. (*Puts the phone down, indignant.*) She's ... she's with him! She's spent the night there! That's disgusting!

(*BERYL gives him an old fashioned look.*)

CHARLES. Have you seen my socks?
BERYL. They're hanging on the light fitting in the kitchen. Don't you remember?
CHARLES. Oh, yes. Yes ...

(*HE heads for the kitchen. SHE follows, wrapping the blanket 'round herself.*)

BERYL. My tights are up there, too.

(*THEY exit. Meanwhile, ARTHUR has continued dithering, as HE looks 'round at the glasses, bottles, etc.*)

ARTHUR. Oh, lor' ... I don't ... I mean, I ... (*Finds a dress and a bra draped over a chair.*) Oh, no ...

DORIS. (*Comes from the bathroom, wrapped in a man's bathrobe. SHE's bright and cheerful.*) Good morning.

ARTHUR. Doris, I don't know what to say ...

DORIS. I hope you don't mind me having a quick shower ... only I felt all sticky after last night.

ARTHUR. (*Reacts.*) I don't remember a thing. Surely it doesn't count, if you don't remember it?

DORIS. What? What don't you remember?

ARTHUR. I don't know, do I?

DORIS. Oh. Well, anyway, I'd just like to say "thank you."

ARTHUR. That's not necessary, Doris.

DORIS. It was very kind of you to let me sleep it off on your settee.

ARTHUR. It was madness! I must have ... Pardon?

DORIS. My legs went. What must you think of me?

ARTHUR. (*Puzzling it through.*) You mean, you slept on the ...? (*Indicates the settee.*)

DORIS. (*Nods.*) You covered me with a blanket. (*Picks up a folded blanket and a pillow from behind the settee.*)

ARTHUR. And I slept up ... (*Huge relief.*) Oh ... aha ... and we didn't ... (*Chuckles, then suddenly wary.*) We didn't, did we?

DORIS. Certainly not! Ooh, Arthur. I'm a married woman.

ARTHUR. Absolutely. So am I. (*Clutches head.*) Ooh ...

DORIS. Oh, I've put some coffee on. I think you need it. Strong and black ... (*Heads for kitchen.*)

ARTHUR. Yes, I think I do. Doris, why haven't you got a hangover?

DORIS. Oh, well ... I think I'm still drunk. Hic! (*Exits to kitchen.*)

(*The front DOORBELL RINGS. ARTHUR moves to answer it, unsteady.*)

ARTHUR. That's a good way to avoid one. Never sober up.

(*HE opens the front door. MISS TROTTER breezes in.*)

MISS TROTTER. Coo-ee! It's only me ...

ARTHUR. Ah! Miss Trott ...

MISS TROTTER. I'm not staying. I just wondered if I could borrow a nutmeg?

ARTHUR. (*Uneasy.*) Er ... yes. I'm not sure where we keep them.

MISS TROTTER. I expect they'll be in your kitchen.

ARTHUR. No! No ... ahaha ... it's un ... (*Arm 'round her, leads her away from kitchen door.*) Ahaha ... Tell me, what's the latest news in the neighborhood?

MISS TROTTER. (*Looks at him, surprised to be asked, then plunges into gossip.*) Well ... the Barracloughs, on the corner, they're rowing again. Some of the neighbors are taking her side and some are taking his ...

ARTHUR. And I expect there'll be a few eccentrics who are minding their own business. (*During all this, ARTHUR contrives to snatch up the dress and bra, etc. and keep them behind his back.*)

MISS TROTTER. Oh, probably. The milkman ... he's parked outside Mrs. Frazer's again. It doesn't take two hours to pay a milk bill ... they must think we're fools! Still, you don't want to stand here and listen to me gossiping ... (*Heads for kitchen, is diverted again.*)

ARTHUR. I do! I do!

MISS TROTTER. Well ... that's about it, really. There's nothing else going on that I know of ...

(*DORIS enters from the kitchen, carrying two cups of coffee. Miss Trotter is not in her line of vision and DORIS doesn't notice her.*)

DORIS. Here we are ... coffee!

ARTHUR. Yes ... erm ... coffee. (*HE sits on the bra/dress etc. in order to hide them.*)

DORIS. I've made an extra cup. I thought you'd like to take it up to Beryl.

ARTHUR. That's very nice of ... (*Take.*) Just a minute! Beryl ...!

DORIS. What about her?

ARTHUR. Where is she? She wasn't in bed when ... when ... She wasn't in bed!

DORIS. No? Oh, dear. I'd better get dressed. Charles will be wondering when I am. I ... (*Sees her.*) Oh, hullo, Miss Trotter.

MISS TROTTER. (*Fascinated.*) Don't mind me. Do carry on.

DORIS. I just ... uh ... popped in to ... to ... Where are my clothes?

ARTHUR. Clothes? I've no idea.

MISS TROTTER. (*Indicates.*) He's sitting on them.

ARTHUR. So I am ... aha ... (*Retrieves them. Hands the bundle to Doris.*) Sorry. I was trying to get the creases out.

DORIS. Thank you. I'll get dressed. Excuse me. (*Exits upstairs to bathroom, with her clothes.*)

ARTHUR. So ...! You were saying about the Barracloughs?

MISS TROTTER. Who?

ARTHUR. The Barracloughs. They're rowing again.

MISS TROTTER. Are they?

ARTHUR. And the milkman was outside Mrs. ... Look, Miss Trotter, I know what this must look like ...

MISS TROTTER. Oh, yes.

ARTHUR. But it's not what you ... Their shower isn't working, you see. So Doris ... Mrs. Summerskill ... popped over to ... to ... borrow ours. Not in the sense of taking it away, but ... but ... to use it. Mainly to shower in. Alone.

MISS TROTTER. And she undressed down here?

ARTHUR. It ... would seem so. Heaven knows why ... I wasn't here watching, or anything. Good lord, no ... Nutmeg!

MISS TROTTER. Who?

ARTHUR. (*Steers her towards the kitchen.*) You came to borrow some. It's on the shelf ... See yourself out the back, will you?

(*SHE exits to kitchen, as the front door opens and BERYL, now dressed, lets herself in with her key. CHARLES, also dressed, is close behind her.*)

BERYL. (*Unabashed.*) Morning, Arthur.

ARTHUR. Where have you been?

CHARLES. Never mind where she's been! What's this about my wife staying the night here?!

ARTHUR. (*Defensive.*) Oh, well now ... nothing happened! She passed out on the settee and ... I covered her with a blanket.

CHARLES. You expect me to believe a cock and bull story like that? (*To Beryl.*) Hah!

(*DORIS enters from the bathroom, now dressed.*)

ARTHUR. It's true! I ... Beryl, where have you been?

BERYL. Oh, that's it. Attack is the best form of defense.

DORIS. Morning, all.

CHARLES. Hah! (*To Arthur.*) She stayed at my place. Just as Doris stayed with you!

DORIS. I slept on the settee.

ARTHUR. And I slept upstairs. It was totally innocent. Just as I'm sure it was with you two.

CHARLES. On the settee? And you upstairs?

ARTHUR. Just as I'm sure it was with you two?

CHARLES. (*Guilty.*) Oh ... yes. Absolutely. Totally innocent.

DORIS. Same as us.

CHARLES. Are you sure about that?

ARTHUR. Oh, dear me. (*Takes Bible from bookcase.*) Look ... here. I swear on the Bible. Totally innocent.

CHARLES. Can't say fairer than that ... What?

(*ARTHUR hands him the Bible, indicates it's his turn.*)

CHARLES. Ah ... very nice. Yes. Morocco leather, if I'm not mistaken ...

DORIS. It's your turn, Charles.

CHARLES. (*Floundering.*) Yes ... what happened to ... to trust between friends? It's a poor lookout if a man can't ... if he's asked to ... unf ... unf ...

BERYL. (*Impatient.*) It's no good, Charlie. It's written all over your face.

CHARLES. Oh. There goes the star witness for the defense.

ARTHUR. (*Stunned.*) You mean ... you and ... you ...?

(*CHARLES and BERYL nod.*)

DORIS. (*Stunned.*) Oh, Charles!

CHARLES. It was only once ...

BERYL. Twice.

CHARLES. Will you leave this to me! (*To Arthur.*) It wasn't planned! It was ... it was that wine of yours ...

DORIS. (*To Beryl.*) How could you? And to think I lent you my big saucepan! (*Tearful. Leans on Arthur.*)

ARTHUR. There, there, there ... I thought we'd been happy together all these years, Beryl.

BERYL. You didn't, did you?

ARTHUR. Well, no. I s'pose not, no.

BERYL. I mean, we never talked to each other.

ARTHUR. (*Bitter.*) We'll have something to talk *about* now, won't we?

DORIS. (*Tearful.*) *And* my omelette pan!

CHARLES. Look, look, don't upset yourself, Doris. I know it's a shock, but we'll probably all have a good laugh about it in a few ... well, perhaps not, but ...

BERYL. It's not the end of the world.

CHARLES. Exactly. Let's be civilized ... pretend it never happened. Nobody else need know ... we can keep it between ourselves ...

MISS TROTTER. (*Pops her head 'round the door to the kitchen.*) Cooeee!

(*Reactions as EVERYBODY sees her. SHE has obviously heard everything. SHE enters the room.*)

MISS TROTTER. Found the nutmeg. (*Shows it.*) Now, let's see if I've got this straight ... (*SHE indicates first Beryl and Charles, then Doris and Arthur, sorting out in her own mind who has stayed the night with whom. Bursting to spread the news, SHE scuttles out of the front door.*) It's a good thing it's only me. Some people might talk. Ooohoo! (*SHE exits.*)

(*A stunned silence. DORIS sits, overwhelmed.*)

BERYL. That's all we need. Mighty mouth's got it. (*To Charles.*) By the time she tells it, I'll have moved in with you.

ARTHUR. Why don't you ? Seeing as how I make you so miserable.

DORIS. Yes! It wouldn't bother me. (*Sees CHARLES' face.*) Well, you don't expect me to come home as though nothing has happened.

CHARLES. It was only a moment of madness...

BERYL. *Two* moments of madness.

DORIS. At least you'll have someone to laugh at your stupid jokes.

CHARLES. (*Wounded.*) Stupid jokes?

DORIS. Putting a frog in my oven gloves. Stupid!

CHARLES. I see. (*To Beryl.*) Well, it's all right with me, if it's all right with you!

BERYL. It's all right with me!

CHARLES. Right! (*Offers her his arm.*)

(*BERYL takes it defiantly.*)

ARTHUR. (*Events are moving too fast for him.*) Just a ... I mean, it's all very well to ... but ... What about Doris?

DORIS. Oh, I'll move in with you.
ARTHUR. Fine. You'll *what?!*

(*Go to BLACK, so that both sets are now in
     darkness.*

Brings LIGHTS on:)

Scene 3

SCENE: Summerskills' living room.

*AT RISE: Early evening of the same day. The
     room now contains suitcases, piles of Beryl's
     clothes draped over the furniture. A hood
     hairdryer, hot rollers, make-up boxes, etc.
     The glasses and bottles of the previous
     evening are still there. CHARLES is just
     staggering through the front door loaded down
     with armfuls of clothes, shoes, boots, etc.
     BERYL close behind him with a small hatbox.*

CHARLES. Good grief, you've got more
clothes than an earthquake appeal.
     BERYL. Mm. You can get the rest tomorrow.
     CHARLES. The rest? (*Drops the clothes on a
chair.*)

BERYL. This is mostly stuff I don't wear. Drinkie-poo?

CHARLES. Scotch, please.

(*Sees SHE's about to pour into a dirty glass from last night.*)

CHARLES. In a clean glass.

BERYL. Ooh, fussy! (*SHE wipes the glass on the hem of one of her dresses, then pours.*)

CHARLES. D'you think ... perhaps ... things have got a little ... out of hand, at all?

BERYL. Well, it'll make a change.

CHARLES. Ye-ess ...

(*DORIS comes from the kitchen carrying several pots and pans. SHE puts them in a cardboard box near the kitchen door. SHE is stony faced.*)

DORIS. (*Calling back.*) Empty the chip pan, I'm taking that. (*To Beryl.*) I'm taking *all* my pots and pans.

BERYL. That's all right. I haven't got any use for 'em.

(*CHARLES looks uncertain.*)

DORIS. *And* my recipes. I'm not having the likes of you doing my haddock and mushroom flan. (*Exits to the kitchen again.*)

BERYL. (*Lights a cigarette.*) I wouldn't know where to start.

CHARLES. Ah, well, you take delicious flaky haddock and tiny button mushrooms ... with some finely grated cheese ...

BERYL. Oh, well, if you know how, *you* can do it.

(*DORIS comes from the kitchen carrying more items of kitchen equipment. ARTHUR, now dressed, close behind her. HE carries more equipment. HE puts it in the cardboard box. Lifts it up. HE is also stony faced.*)

DORIS. (*To Beryl.*) I've left you a dustpan and brush ... but there's no book of instructions.

CHARLES. Doris ...

DORIS. Don't you talk to me. Come on, Arthur.

ARTHUR. Yes. (*To Charles, wounded dignity.*) I've got to say this. You ... you are a double-crossing, womanizing snake in the grass ... An untrustworthy, good-for-nothing lecher!

CHARLES. Are we working tomorrow?

ARTHUR. Hah!

(*HE exits, slamming the front door. DORIS has preceded him.*)

BERYL. (*Sits.*) He's upset about something. I can always tell.

CHARLES. (*Sits.*) I blame him for this whole mess, y'know.

BERYL. Why? He hasn't done anything.

CHARLES. Exactly! He's trying to make me feel guilty.

BERYL. You *are* guilty.

CHARLES. So are you.

BERYL. You're right. I blame him, too. I mean, if he and Doris had done what we did, we'd have all been quits.

CHARLES. Could have forgiven each other. No thought for others, some people.

BERYL. Selfish.

CHARLES. Would you like another drink before dinner?

BERYL. Dinner?

CHARLES. Well, yes ... dinner. I mean, it's getting on and we didn't have any lunch.

BERYL. Oh, I expect I could manage cheese on toast.

CHARLES. Chee ...? But, Doris always does a chicken casserole on Monday.

BERYL. (*Sexy.*) Cheese on toast ... followed by an early night. (*SHE exits to the kitchen.*)

CHARLES. (*Keen.*) Oohoo...! (*Swigs his drink.*) Even better! (*HE follows her.*)

(*LIGHTS cross-fade and up on Greys' living room. Night. The room is now tidy. DORIS enters from the kitchen, followed by ARTHUR. SHE carries a casserole dish. HE*)

has place mats, knives, forks, etc. During the
following, HE sets the table and SHE bustles
in and out of the kitchen, bringing in
vegetable dishes, etc.)

ARTHUR. I suppose we are doing the right
thing? I mean, there's a word for it. A rather ugly
word.

DORIS. What, eating chicken casserole?

ARTHUR. No, no ... wife swapping.

DORIS. Oh, it's hardly that, is it? That sounds
... well, rude.

ARTHUR. Not really. I mean ... (*Sniffs.*)
Oooh ... Oh ... Magnificent. I've almost forgotten
what food smells like.

DORIS. My mother used to say all you need to
keep a man happy is good cooking.

ARTHUR. Yes. Well ... not quite. (*Ill at*
ease.) Y'see, there is *one* thing we haven't
discussed ...

DORIS. What's that?

ARTHUR. Well ... the, erm ... not to put too
fine a point on it, to come straight to it and not ...
uh, go all 'round the houses ... the ... uh ...
sleeping arrangements.

DORIS. Oh, I'll have the spare room.

ARTHUR. Ah. Only I was thinking ... with
her over there ... with him ... and you and I over
here, with me ... I thought ... well, we'd ...
perhaps, you know ... tit for tat.

DORIS. How d'you mean?

ARTHUR. Well, they're tatting ... perhaps you and I should ...

DORIS. Oh, Arthur. I don't think I'm ready for that. Just because they do it, doesn't mean we have to.

ARTHUR. No, we don't *have* to, but ... I thought you might *like* to.

DORIS. Oh, no. I mean ... It isn't even Saturday.

ARTHUR. No. No ...

(*SHE exits to the kitchen again, HE follows her out.*

LIGHTS cross-fade and up on Summerskills' living room. Night. CHARLES is just coming downstairs. HE wears pyjamas and dressing gown. HE calls back up the stairs.)

CHARLES. How much longer are you gonna be in that bathroom, Beryl?!

BERYL. (*Offstage.*) Just making myself beautiful for you.

CHARLES. I'm not that fussy, y'know. I am used to Doris.

BERYL. Charlie ...

CHARLES. What?

BERYL. Is there any particular perfume that turns you on?

CHARLES. Er ... you haven't got Christian Dior's "Roast Beef and Yorkshire" have you?

(*During the above, HE has been rummaging among nearly empty bowls of crisps and nuts left over from the previous night. HE's eating the crumbs.*)

    BERYL. Don't tell me you're still hungry?

    CHARLES. I'm starving!

(*BERYL enters, coming downstairs in a sexy negligee. SHE poses.*)

    BERYL. You should have eaten your cheese on toast.

    CHARLES. It was all soggy. After it caught fire and you threw the cocoa over it.

    BERYL. I'll take your mind off food.

    CHARLES. I can't ... (*See her. Reacts.*) Aha...

    BERYL. D'you like it? (*Climbs onto his lap.*)

    CHARLES. Very nice.

    BERYL. I used your lemon bath salts ... hope you don't mind.

    CHARLES. Oh, no. (*SHE snuggles up to him.*) My word, you smell ... mm ... delicious.

    BERYL. Well, here we are, then.

    CHARLES. Mmm. D'you know what I've got on my mind?

    BERYL. (*Sexy.*) I think I do.

    CHARLES. Doris' homemade lemon meringue! (*Stands, tipping her off his lap and heads for the kitchen.*) I'm sure she left some in the biscuit tin!

(*SHE flings a cushion at him.*)

CURTAIN

ACT II

Scene 1

SCENE: *Summerskills' living room.*

AT RISE: *One week later. Morning. The room now has the untidyness that seems to go with Beryl. SHE is sitting, painting her fingernails. SHE wears a dressing gown and is singing happily to herself.*

BERYL. I didn't sleep a wink last night ... La-di-dadee ... (*Etc.*)

(*CHARLES enters from the hall. HE has aged in a week and looks careworn and tired. HE wears creased pyjamas and dressing gown.*)

CHARLES. Ooh ... Ooh ...

BERYL. Morning, Charlie. You finally got out of bed, then?

CHARLES. Aah ... I haven't been sleeping too well, I think I've done my back in ...

BERYL. If you're making a cuppa tea, I'll have one.

CHARLES. Yes ... just give me a minute to ... to get my strength back. (*Sits heavily.*) D'you know where my shirts are, Beryl?

BERYL. What shirts?

CHARLES. The one I put in the laundry basket.

BERYL. Oh, them. They're in the laundry basket.

CHARLES. Ah ... Only Doris usually washes and irons them for me.

BERYL. (*Doubtful.*) Ooh, I don't think she'll do that now.

CHARLES. No.

BERYL. Be too much to ask.

CHARLES. Yes.

BERYL. Oh, we've run out of cornflakes, but it doesn't matter, 'cause the milk's gone sour.

CHARLES. Beryl, erm ... how can I put this ... I cannot function properly on an empty stomach.

BERYL. I gave you beans on toast.

CHARLES. That was Tuesday. I've sort of fallen into the habit of eating every day.

BERYL. And what about that stew I made last night?

CHARLES. Is *that* what it was?

BERYL. That went down quick enough.

CHARLES. It came up even quicker ...

BERYL. I'm no good in the kitchen. I never was. I'm good in the bedroom ...

CHARLES. Perhaps you could cook up there ... (*Holds stomach.*) Oohh ...

BERYL. You're beginning to sound like Arthur. These hands were not made for cooking and washing up.

CHARLES. You've got rubber gloves, haven't you? Or did we have them for dinner on Monday?

BERYL. (*Changing tack.*) Are you and Arthur speaking to each other yet?

CHARLES. I passed him in the High Street yesterday. We exchanged a couple of words. Well, they were both his, actually.

BERYL. You've got to start working together sometime. If only for the money. I mean, he's stopped my housekeeping, now that I'm not keeping his house. I, er ... I got my monthly account at the hairdressers. It's on your desk.

CHARLES. (*Uneasy, HE gets up. Crosses to the desk.*) Monthly account? Doris never ... (*Finds bill. Aghast.*) Aagh! When did they gold plate your hair?

BERYL. The others are from the dress shop, the manicurist ...

CHARLES. What?

BERYL. (*Slightly arch.*) You want me to look beautiful for you ...

CHARLES. Yes ... but ... these are for last month! You were looking beautiful for Arthur. He can pay 'em.

BERYL. Charlie ... you're not starting to have any regrets, are you?

CHARLES. No! No ... No. (*Finds another bill.*) Dear God! You've bought a shoe shop!

BERYL. They're not *all* big bills.

CHARLES. No, no. There's one here for less than two pounds. Groceries! Haha!

BERYL. I'll tell you what I'll do. Just to cheer you up. I'll go to the hairdressers, I'll have a manicure ...

CHARLES. It's not working so far.

BERYL. ... But first, I'll get dressed. You gonna come and help me? (*SHE takes his hand, pulls him towards the stairs.*)

CHARLES. Uh ... my back! (*Clutches his spine.*)

(*As THEY exit from sight.*

LIGHTS cross-fade and rise on Greys' living room. Still early morning. The room is now neat and tidy. Fresh flowers, everything in its place. DORIS is just coming from the kitchen. SHE's carrying a heaped breakfast plate. SHE is fully dressed. ARTHUR, also fully dressed, is just coming from the hall with a newspaper.)

DORIS. Here we are ... bacon, sausages, kidneys, liver, fried potatoes, mushrooms and scrambled egg.

ARTHUR. (*Doubtful.*) Ooh, I don't think I could manage all that.

DORIS. 'Course you can. You need a bit of flesh on you.

ARTHUR. Oh, I do, I do. It's been a week, Doris.

DORIS. How d'you mean?

ARTHUR. Oh, nothing. (*Picks up knife and fork. Eyes his heaped plate, daunted.*) Erm ...

DORIS. Now, what would you like for lunch?

ARTHUR. Can ... can I finish my breakfast first?

DORIS. No hurry. It'll be a few minutes before the waffles are ready.

ARTHUR. W-waffles?

DORIS. Mm ... (*Sits opposite him. Squints behind her at a picture on the wall.*) ... with maple syrup and cream. Does that picture look straight to you?

ARTHUR. I don't know. I can't see over my plate.

DORIS. There's more toast, if you want it.

(*SHE gets up and straightens the picture. Flicks imaginary dust off things with her apron.*)

ARTHUR. No! No, thank you. (*Begins to eat, without enthusiasm.*) Are you, er ... sleeping well?

DORIS. Like a log. It's nice to have a bed all to yourself, isn't it?

ARTHUR. (*Non-committal.*) Mmm ... Is there anything you ... miss ... since you moved in?

DORIS. Well, yes ... I do miss Rumpetty.

ARTHUR. (*Unsure.*) Erm ... Well, we're all human.

DORIS. He's not. He's a cat. Used to come in for a saucer of milk every morning.

ARTHUR. Oh, that Rumpetty. I was thinking more of ... married life.

DORIS. Well, we've almost got that here, haven't we?

ARTHUR. Almost, Doris, *almost*. Not quite. And all this red meat isn't helping.

DORIS. You need to take your mind off it. It's time you started working again.

ARTHUR. How can I work with him, when he's got my wife?!

DORIS. You've got his.

ARTHUR. Not in the same way he's got mine! Man cannot live by bread, bacon, sausages, kidneys, liver, fried potatoes, mushrooms and scrambled egg alone!

DORIS. Let's not play word games, Arthur. Let's give it its real name. You're talking about Mr. Naughties aren't you?

ARTHUR. Unless he's another cat, yes!

DORIS. I don't think we should. It could spoil our friendship.

ARTHUR. That's what marriage *is*! Friendship gone wrong.

DORIS. We're not married.

ARTHUR. Yes, we are!

DORIS. Not to each other!

ARTHUR. Oh, well, if you're going to split hairs ... It's not working, Doris.

DORIS. Neither are you. You haven't sharpened your pencil once this week.

ARTHUR. That's what I've just been saying.

DORIS. You've signed a contract. And you haven't got a single idea in your head ... apart from one. You can't do it on your own, Arthur.

ARTHUR. I haven't got a lot of choice.

DORIS. You'll have to start writing with Charles sooner or late. Swallow your pride.

ARTHUR. I couldn't eat another thing. (*Pushes his plate away.*) And I can't forgive him.

DORIS. He can't forgive you, either

ARTHUR. I haven't done anything!

DORIS. Exactly! That puts him in a very awkward situation.

ARTHUR. Perhaps if I apologized?

DORIS. For what?

ARTHUR. I don't know! I'm riddled with guilt and I don't know why!

DORIS. Phone him. (*Puts phone in front of him.*)

ARTHUR. Oh, no. No, no. I do not want to speak to him.

DORIS. You don't have to speak to him. Just phone him.

ARTHUR. (*Folds arms.*) No!

DORIS. Then I will. (*Starts to dial.*)

ARTHUR. I've got absolutely nothing to say to him and you can tell him I said so. No, don't ... that'll be saying something.

(*LIGHTS rise on Summerskills' living room. CHARLES, now casually dressed in rather rumpled clothes, is coming from the kitchen with the vacuum cleaner.*)

CHARLES. Ooh, the dust on this thing.

(*The TELEPHONE RINGS.*)

CHARLES. (*Sarcastic, calling to kitchen.*) No need to rush ... I'll get it. (*Picking up phone.*) Hullo ...
DORIS. (*To phone.*) Is that you?
CHARLES. Hullo, Doris. What are you cooking?
DORIS. Eh? Oh, I've just done breakfast. Bacon, sausages, kidneys, liver, fried potatoes, mushrooms and scrambled ...
CHARLES. Oh, God! I can smell it! (*Sniffs at phone in ecstasy.*)
DORIS. I'm calling for Arthur ...
CHARLES. He's not here.
DORIS. I know that. He's here. Eating his bacon, sausage, kidn ...
CHARLES. Is that why you called? To torture me!

ARTHUR. Tell him I never want to see his rat-like face again! May he rot in hell!

DORIS. He says when are you getting together to work again?

ARTHUR. (*To self.*) That lost something in translation.

CHARLES. (*Surprised.*) You mean ... he's prepared to let bygones be bygones? And go back to work?

ARTHUR. I'm not working with him until pigs grow wings and the moon turns blue!

DORIS. Under the right conditions, yes.

CHARLES. I'm willing if he is. (*Towards the kitchen, for Beryl's benefit.*) I've got several shoe shops to support!

DORIS. He'll be right 'round. (*Phone down.*)

CHARLES. Fine. What are you cooking for dinner tonight ... Doris? (*Cradles phone. Looks thoughtful.*) Hmm ...

(*Over in the Grey's living room, ARTHUR folds his arms, looking determined.*)

ARTHUR. I am not going. No way. Out of the question. I am not working with him again. Oh, no, no, no ...

DORIS. Oh, stop waffling, Arthur ... (*A thought.*) Waffles! (*Heads for kitchen, taking his plate with her.*)

ARTHUR. (*Groans.*) Ooh ... no, Doris. No! I've got to go and *work,* Doris!

(*ARTHUR heads for the front door. Takes his coat from the hall rack and exits.*

Summerskills' living room. BERYL enters from the kitchen.)

BERYL. There! Don't say I never do things around the house.

CHARLES. Um ...? What? What have you done?

BERYL. This cat came in. I gave it a saucer o' milk.

CHARLES. Rumpetty? (*HE begins to tidy up, dust, polish, as he talks.*)

BERYL. Ooh, you'll have to be quick. I've got a hairdressing appointment.

CHARLES. What? No, the cat! (*Clutches his back.*) That's his name. Besides, Arthur's coming 'round. To work. If he found us ... at it, on the rug, he might think it less than ... tactful.

BERYL. Ooh, yes ... I hadn't thought of that.

CHARLES. (*Thoughtful.*) It won't be an easy day, as it is. It may be on his mind, anyway.

BERYL. What about him and Doris? Don't tell me they've spent the past week playing tiddlywinks.

CHARLES. It's very likely. At least she enjoys tiddlywinks.

BERYL Oh, come on, Charlie. She's a woman, he's a man.

CHARLES. No, no, no. Not Doris. I know her
... (*Dawning doubt.*) She's not ... she wouldn't ...
Would she? I mean ... he'd be getting good food as
well as ... That's not fair!

BERYL. He's quite keen on it, Arthur. For a
popgun.

CHARLES. Ah, but she *isn't*, you see. She
approaches it with all the excitement of a cold
semolina pudding ...

BERYL. Hm?

CHARLES. Cold semolina pudding.

BERYL. I think she left some in the fridge.

CHARLES. No, I ... (*Keen.*) Really? (*Exits to
the kitchen, enthusiastic.*)

(*The front DOORBELL RINGS. BERYL crosses to
open it. ARTHUR steps in, looking bitter.*)

BERYL. Hullo, Arthur.

ARTHUR. Are you talking to me?

BERYL. No. The hallstand. I call it Arthur,
because it never does anything exciting. Come in
... sit down on "Fred." (*Indicates armchair.*)

ARTHUR. Jezebel!

BERYL. No, that's the desk.

ARTHUR. You don't care, do you, Beryl?

BERYL. What d'you want me to say? What's
done is done. It was just one moment of weakness,
that's all.

ARTHUR. (*Hope.*) You mean ... it *was* just
the once? You and ... haven't been ... since?

BERYL. Oh, all right ... a dozen moments of weakness ...

ARTHUR. Hah!

(*Enter CHARLES from the kitchen, eating cold semolina from a bowl with enjoyment.*)

CHARLES. Mm ... mm ... a little mouldy, but very acceptable. (*Sees Arthur. Unsure.*) Ah! Good morning.

ARTHUR. Don't try and soft talk me. I've only come 'round here for two reasons. We have a contract ... and I couldn't face any more waffles.

CHARLES. Waffles! Hot, crispy waffles!

BERYL. Oh, gawd. I'm going to get my hair done ... (*Picks up handbag, etc.*)

CHARLES. With cream and maple syrup ...

BERYL. I might pop into the boutique afterwards.

ARTHUR. Well, don't send *me* the bill.

BERYL. Don't worry. Charlie's taking care of all that.

ARTHUR. Oh. There's a sale on at the fur shop. Do a nice line in mink jackets ... next to the jewelers.

(*CHARLES splutters on his semolina.*)

BERYL. Oh, I'll look in. Now, for goodness sake, you two, be sensible. Try and get on with each other. Above all ... be tactful. 'Bye, lover ...

(*Waves at Charles and exits through the front door.*)

(*ARTHUR scowls at Charles.*)

CHARLES. (*Clears throat.*) Ahaha ... So, er ... Beryl and I, we ...

ARTHUR. I don't want to know. I am here to work. Nothing else. I am not interested in your grubby personal life.

CHARLES. Fine, fine.

ARTHUR. I just want to pick up, where we left off. We need a fresh, original idea. Something with style and sophistication ...

CHARLES. (*Crosses to desk.*) How about ...?

ARTHUR. That does not involve Wigan, knicker factories, or anyone called Mr. Bloody.

CHARLES. Fine. (*Crumples notes he has picked up. Drops them in the wastebin. Whistles tunelessly.*)

ARTHUR. I, for one, am not going to make any reference to what has happened this past week.

CHARLES. Fine. (*Sits at desk.*)

ARTHUR. (*Paces, controlling his agitation.*) Some people would be bitter. Not me. I can push it to the back of my mind. And work. I can do that.

CHARLES. Good. Very good.

ARTHUR. And it takes strength of character ... believe me ... to forget all about it, when somebody's pinched your wife!

CHARLES. Oh, it does. I can only admire the way you're doing it.

ARTHUR. Light ... frothy ... stylish ... That's the sort of comedy we ought to be writing!

CHARLES. Ah, work ... yes.

ARTHUR. Something with a bit of class ...

CHARLES. I've no objection to that. Let's see ... our main character could be a ... Man about town ... a boulevardier ... M'sieur Sanguinaire .. owner of ... erm ... Un Fabrique de Directoire.

ARTHUR. Is that French for what I think it is?

CHARLES. It was worth a try.

ARTHUR. Forget it!

CHARLES. Fine. Light ... sophisticated ... um ...

ARTHUR. Um ...

(*THEY ponder.*)

CHARLES. Um ... Are you and Doris ... not that I could object, if you were ... under the circumstances ... hitting it off, at all?

ARTHUR. Me and Doris?

CHARLES. In the ... Mister Naughties department, I mean.

ARTHUR. Is it any of your business?

CHARLES. (*Thinks about it.*) Yes.

ARTHUR. Yes, I suppose it is. (*Sits.*)

CHARLES. Because if you were ... and it would be perfectly understandable ... what with

Beryl and I at it, like ... uh ... sometimes twice a
... (*See ARTHUR's expression. Changes tack.*)
Light and frothy ... light and frothy ...

ARTHUR. No, we are not!

CHARLES. Ah, good. (*Relieved, HE smiles
despite himself.*) Um ... aha ... good. I mean, it
would have been all *right* ... considering that
Beryl and I ...

ARTHUR. Will you shut up!

CHARLES. Sorry. I, er ... I haven't had a
decent meal for a week, you know.

ARTHUR. (*Sarcastic.*) Oh, dear. Oh, dear.

CHARLES. I was wondering ... I know it's a
lot to ask, but ... if you ever have any surplus ...
cakes ... scones ... or a little of Doris' apple
turnover ... Rather than let it go stale ... (*Sees
ARTHUR's disbelieving face.*) Erm ... another
time, perhaps.

(*ARTHUR stands.*)

CHARLES. What are you doing?

ARTHUR. I'm going to the toilet. It seems
preferable to hitting you. (*Exits to toilet, closing
door.*)

CHARLES. (*Calling.*) Is it something I said?
You're very touchy this morning.

(*HE takes the crumpled sheaf of notes from the
wastebin and smooths it out. A ring at the
DOORBELL. HE crosses to open the front*

door. MAURICE breezes in, carrying briefcase, airline bag, duty free bag.)

CHARLES. Maurice! Come in. Make yourself comfortable ... hang upside down from something.

MAURICE. Just come from the airport. Thought I'd stop by to pick up the script.

CHARLES. Ah ... not quite finished, Maurice. Needs a little polishing.

MAURICE. What page are you on?

CHARLES. Well ... one. Almost.

MAURICE. You mean you haven't started it?

CHARLES. We haven't been able to come up with a halfway decent idea.

MAURICE. That's never stopped you before. It's only television, for god's sake. Now, look here, Charles ... I'm going to give you a good talking to ... *(Wags finger.)*

CHARLES. How was New York? And Tony's play? And the Awards?

MAURICE. You're trying to change the subject.

CHARLES. Yes. Is it working?

MAURICE. *(Thinks about it.)* Ye-ess, it is. *(Sits, keen.)* Fantastic opening night ... rave reviews ... twelve curtain calls ...

CHARLES. I've changed my mind. Give me a good talking to.

MAURICE. And his other play won a Tony award! Yes! That's three he's got!

CHARLES. Another seven, he can open a bowling alley.

MAURICE. Absolutely fabulous trip, spoilt only by one thing ...

CHARLES. What?

MAURICE. Coming back here and finding that you two have spent the past week pulling your wretched plonkers. Where's Arthur?

CHARLES. He's in the toilet.

MAURICE. There's no time for that! What's the matter with the pair of you?

CHARLES. Well, actually ... (*Glances towards toilet, wondering whether to confide in Maurice.*) I did have one or two ideas, but Arthur wasn't ... er ... It's been a difficult week, Maurice.

MAURICE. Tell me.

CHARLES. I ... I'm not sure I ...

MAURICE. I am your friend.

(*CHARLES looks at him in astonishment.*)

MAURICE. All right, your agent.

CHARLES. Yes ... um. I'd like your advice, Maurice ...

(*Sits beside him. During the following, casually helps himself to Maurice's duty-free whisky.*)

CHARLES. Imagine ... two married couples ... known each other for years ... One husband a dull, cloddish type ... (*Glances towards toilet.*) ... married to a sexpot who can't cook.

MAURICE. Ye-es ...

CHARLES. Now, the other chap ... a good looking, witty, sophisticated fellow, irresistible to women ... is married to an excellent cook, but a non-started in the nookie stakes ...

MAURICE. They're married to the wrong ones.

CHARLES. Yes. So ... they swap wives, you see. But now they're beginning to wonder if they've made a mistake. (*HIS back twinges.*) Ooh ... Perhaps the grass isn't greener.

MAURICE. (*Stands, paces for a moment, thoughtful.*) Mmm ... I *like* it!

CHARLES. What?

MAURICE. It'll make a good first episode.

CHARLES. No ... (*Stands.*)

MAURICE. Yes! It's just the sort of stuff that gets the ratings. It's dirty!

CHARLES. You don't understand ... I was saying that it ... it actually ... you see ... (*HIS eyes light up.*) It is, isn't it?

MAURICE. Absolutely! Could run for years.

CHARLES. (*Mind racing.*) Yes! Yes, it's not bad at all.

MAURICE. Is there anything more? What do they do for a living?

CHARLES. (*Notices his sheaf of notes.*) I ... we thought one of them might ... own a knicker factory.

(HE has his back to the toilet. ARTHUR enters, catching the last few words.)

ARTHUR. What? What are you telling him?

MAURICE. He's just told me the idea! It'll work. It'll work!

ARTHUR. Oh, no, no, no. Not that one!

MAURICE. It's got a lot going for it. More than a touch of sex ... wife swapping ...

ARTHUR. Wife ... swapping?

(HE looks at CHARLES, who looks innocent.)

MAURICE. The wife who can't cook ... the other one no good in bed ...

ARTHUR. Er, Charles ... a word ...

MAURICE. The good looking, witty husband ... the other one dull and cloddish.

ARTHUR. "Dull and cloddish!"

CHARLES. I wouldn't quite describe him that way, Maurice.

MAURICE. But you just did.

ARTHUR. You've told Maurice? Everything?

CHARLES. Everything. *(Meaningfully.)* The idea for the new series.

MAURICE. One small snag, boys. Is it ... believable? That sort of thing wouldn't happen in real life, would it?

(CHARLES and ARTHUR look at each other.)

CHARLES and ARTHUR. Um ... er ... oooh
...

MAURICE. Still, it's only television.

CHARLES. Exactly!

ARTHUR. Just a minute! No, no. I do not want ten million people watching this on their screens!

CHARLES. Twelve million, if we get the right slot.

ARTHUR. It's bad enough with Miss Trotter spreading it 'round the neighborhood!

MAURICE. Who's Miss Trotter?

ARTHUR. The local gossip!

CHARLES. Oh, yes ... very good idea, Arthur! We'll work her in! (*Starts to lead Maurice towards the door.*) He's getting excited now ... best leave us to it.

MAURICE. Quite, yes. Press on! Get the old joke factory going. Churn 'em out ... (*Looks at his watch – to Arthur.*) Oh, do give my regards to Beryl.

CHARLES. I certainly will.

MAURICE. (*To Charles.*) And Doris.

ARTHUR. I'll do that.

(*MAURICE does a take, then is eased out of the door.*)

CHARLES. 'Bye, Maurice. 'Bye. (*Shuts door, returns.*) Phew ...

ARTHUR. Are you out of your mind?! I'm not having my private life paraded in public! (*Indicates television.*)

CHARLES. Nobody will know it's *us!* We'll set it in Wi ... somewhere up north. We'll make your character lively and amusing! That'll fool 'em.

ARTHUR. Charming!

CHARLES. No-o ... that's going too far. And, if it'll set your mind at rest, we can change the names.

ARTHUR. (*Sour.*) It'd help!

CHARLES. (*Appealing.*) Arthur ... Arthur ...

ARTHUR. You can't call them both "Arthur."

CHARLES. No, I ... tch! A lot of writers draw on their own lives.

ARTHUR. *I* never have.

CHARLES. That's because it's been too bloody boring up until now.

ARTHUR. I see.

CHARLES. I'm sorry. Look, it would work. You have to admit that it's a funny situation.

ARTHUR. Funny?

CHARLES. (*Backtracking.*) Well, not "funny," exactly. It has its humorous side ... er ... well, not "humorous" ... it's more ... or ... not so much "amusing" as ... well, "tragic" I suppose ... in a funny way. Well, not "funny," exactly ... would you like a cup of coffee?

ARTHUR. (*Stands. Heads for front door.*) I came 'round here on the understanding we wouldn't talk about what's happened. Now you want to sit down and write a comedy about it. Well, the answer's "No!" NO!

(*ARTHUR exits through the front door. CHARLES calls after him.*)

CHARLES. We could write it. Light, sophisticated, frothy ... A touch of class ...

ARTHUR. (*Returns immediately.*) Ah, now ... that way it *could* work!

CHARLES. Good man. (*Crosses to desk, rubbing his hands.*) Put the coffee on ... Now then ... sophisticated. Mmmm. That suggests more of an affluent suburb, rather than Wigan itself ...

ARTHUR. (*Stops at kitchen door. Firmly.*) Mayfair!

CHARLES. What?

ARTHUR. If we're doing it, we're doing it *my* way. It's in Mayfair ... amongst the smart set. (*Exits to kitchen, leaving the door ajar.*)

CHARLES. (*Calls.*) In the 1930s.

ARTHUR. (*Offstage.*) Why 1930s?

CHARLES. Because your idea of sophistication is sixty years out of date!

ARTHUR. (*Offstage.*) Where's the coffee?

CHARLES. There's some on the floor, by the fridge ... (*Follows him to kitchen door. Calls through.*) It's true, Arthur. What do you know about ... (*Scorn.*) "the smart set?" Let's face it, you are working class. Nothing to be ashamed of, but your background is pure yobbo ...

(*A cabbage comes flying out of the kitchen door, aimed at Charles. HE catches it, staggers back.*)

CHARLES. I see. It's a battle of intellects, is it? (*Moves back to desk.*) All right ... we'll try it your way. It won't work, but we'll try it. (*Picks up clipboard and pencil. Calls towards kitchen.*) And I can imagine what it'll be like!

(*Blackout. Beat. LIGHTS up slowly on Greys' living room.*
It is night. ARTHUR is just coming down the stairs. HE wears a long (too long) dressing gown and cravat. HE wields a long ivory cigarette holder.)

ARTHUR. (*Calls in exaggerated upper class accent.*) Persephone, darling. We shall be frightfully, frightfully late, you know.
CHARLES. (*Walking into set.*) See! I told you it wouldn't work!
ARTHUR. (*Normal voice. Annoyed.*) Do you mind?! I've hardly started!
CHARLES. Carry on ... if you must. (*Moves back to desk area. Watches.*)
ARTHUR. Thank you. (*Accent. To kitchen.*) ... frightfully, frightfully late.

(*BERYL enters from the kitchen. SHE wears a tiara and ball gown. Long white gloves. SHE also has an ivory cigarette holder. SHE carries a silver candelabra, complete with lit candles.*)

BERYL. (*Exaggerated upper class.*) Don't be impatient, Sir Arthur. I'm just setting the table. (*Drops candelabra on table.*) There! (*Exits to kitchen.*)

ARTHUR. Spiffing. (*Crosses to sideboard where HE takes out several boxes of holiday slides, a projector, folded screen, etc. HE holds a slide up to the light.*) Private viewing of our holiday slides tonight ... at Sir Charles Lecher's penthouse

(*BERYL returns carrying a large covered silver salver.*)

ARTHUR. Ah, high tea. What are we having?

BERYL. Beluga caviar and stuffed quails in aspic ... (*Takes lid off salver.*) ... pot of tea and bread and butter for two.

ARTHUR. Again? How boring. (*Sits. Begins to eat.*) Tch ... Persephone, you've burned the caviar!

BERYL. Then next time, Sir Arthur, you can fry it yourself. (*Offers bottle.*) H.P. Sauce?

ARTHUR. Merci.

CHARLES. (*Moves into scene.*) Hold it! Hold it!

(*BERYL freezes.*)

CHARLES. H.P. Sauce? With stuffed quails in aspic?

ARTHUR. (*Normal voice.*) What's wrong with that?

CHARLES. The smart set prefer Daddie's Favourite.

ARTHUR. Do they? Oh, well ... thank you. I'll fix that.

CHARLES. Always happy to help. Keep going ... (*Moves back to desk, sniggering.*)

BERYL. (*Offers bottle.*) Daddie's Favourite?

ARTHUR. Naturally. Merci.

BERYL. Anything for you ... you're so damned handsome and dashing.

ARTHUR. How true. I can't eat any more (*Stands, heads for kitchen with salver.*) I shall toss it to the borzois ...

BERYL. If you'd care for dessert, there's bread and jam in a champagne sauce.

ARTHUR. I think not. (*Exits to kitchen grandly. An exit spoiled as HE trips over his too long dressing gown.*)

(*The front DOORBELL CHIMES "A Room With a View."*)

BERYL. (*Heading for door.*) Ah ... cheap music. It's so potent. (*Opens door.*)

(*MISS TROTTER steps regally into the room SHE is dressed in something stunning, white gloves, tiara, lorgnette.*)

MISS TROTTER. Lady Persephone ... I shan't stay. I wondered if I might borrow a cup of truffles? (*All in one languid breath.*) Have you heard about Viscount Newton's boy? Got a gel from Fortunum and Mason's into trouble ...

BERYL. How boring for him ... (*Crosses to sideboard.*)

MISS TROTTER. Quite. And Lord Johnson's under footman was caught stealing his solid good cycle clips ...

(*Enter ARTHUR from the kitchen.*)

MISS TROTTER. Ah ... Sir Arthur ... handsome and dashing.

ARTHUR. The Marchioness of Trotter ... how are you?

MISS TROTTER. I'm my usual self.

ARTHUR. How boring for you.

MISS TROTTER. Rumor has it that the archbishop has had his lower limb over his parlor maid. But you'll have missed all this, being on the Cote d'Azure, in France, of course ...

ARTHUR. Of course.

MISS TROTTER. On holiday with your friends.

ARTHUR. Ah, yes, my friends ... the weak, spineless Sir Charles Lecher, who is so envious of me because I'm so handsome and dashing ...

CHARLES. (*Entering set.*) Arthur ...

(*MISS TROTTER freezes.*)

ARTHUR. (*Normal.*) Now what?

CHARLES. What's all this "Sir Charles Lecher" stuff?

ARTHUR. Nothing wrong with that. It's spelt with two 'L' s...

CHARLES. Oh. That's all right, then ... (*Back to the desk.*)

ARTHUR. Where was I ...? Oh, yes, I was being ... (*Upper class accent.*) ... handsome and dashing.

(*BERYL returns from sideboard, carrying a salver.*)

MISS TROTTER. What's this?

BERYL. Truffles. I keep a few for the tradesman.

MISS TROTTER. Thank you. Au revoir.

ARTHUR. Adieu ...

MISS TROTTER. (*Heading for door.*) A bientot ...

ARTHUR. Bonne chance ...

MISS TROTTER. A votre sante ...

ARTHUR. Escargot ...

MISS TROTTER. Defense de fumer! (*Exits, closing front door.*)

ARTHUR. (*To Beryl.*) Ah, the language of diplomacy.

BERYL. Shouldn't we be off?

ARTHUR. Yes. (*Crosses to wine cupboard, opens door.*) I promised I'd take a few bottles of Chateau Sir Arthur ... from our vineyard on the Cote d'Azure, in France, of course. (*Selects bottle.*)

BERYL. Of course.

ARTHUR. But, before we go ... I dashed off a song this morning ... (*Sits at piano.*) ... for you.

BERYL. Oh, Sir Arthur.

(*SHE poses at piano, as ARTHUR plays a tinkly tune.*)

ARTHUR. (*Sings.*)
Springtime in Mayfair,
The weather's set to stay fair.
The sun in Belgravia,
Is on his best behaviour.

(*BERYL picks up the sheet music from the piano and sings along with him.*)

ARTHUR and BERYL.
Hand in hand down Rotten Row
Each debutante walks with her beau,

(*SHE tosses away the sheet music, she knows it
    now.*)

ARTHUR and BERYL.
Behind the shrubs for "Tally Ho!"
It's Mayfair in the Spring.

    CHARLES. Jesus wept ...
    BERYL. It's so ... so brittle.
    ARTHUR. It *is* brittle, isn't it?
    BERYL. And yet ... tender.
    ARTHUR. (*Sings.*)
Down Piccadilly,
Each feller picks a filly.
'Neath his grey topper,
His thoughts are quite improper.

(*THEY go into a duet on the chorus.*)

    ARTHUR and BERYL. (*Sing.*)
The nightingales in Berkeley Square,
Are making sure they get their share,
Like knives, they're at it, everywhere.
It's Mayfair in the Spring!

(*CHARLES, unable to stand it any more, walks
    across and into the set.*

Lose desk SPOTLIGHT.

BERYL freezes.)

CHARLES. Hold it! I told you it wouldn't work your way!

ARTHUR. (*Normal voice.*) What? What's the matter? (*Stands, moves away from the piano. It CONTINUES TO PLAY.*) This is the way I want to ... (*Bangs piano. IT STOPS playing.*) You think it's *too* sophisticated?

CHARLES. No-o ... Let me put this ... tactfully ... diplomatically ... uh ... no, I can't. It's a load of codswallop!

ARTHUR. Oh, that's nice.

CHARLES. Let's start again ...

(*The piano BEGINS TO PLAY of its own accord.*)

BERYL. (*Sings.*)
Springtime in Mayfair,
The weather's set to ...

(*ARTHUR bangs the piano. IT STOPS.*)

ARTHUR. Persephone!! "Exits Stage Right to ... to fry more caviar!"

CHARLES. Taking that stuff with her!

(*HE indicates the candelabra and the platter. SHE picks them up, exits to the kitchen with them. Still singing.*)

BERYL.
The weather's set to stay fair ... (*Exits.*)

(*ARTHUR peels off his dressing gown, cravat, etc. Underneath he's dressed as usual. Lose topclothes behind settee.*)

CHARLES.   And   *that*   is   your   idea   of sophistication.
ARTHUR. All right. All right. How do *you* want it? I know how you want to do it. You want to set it in Wigan!
CHARLES.   (*Snaps   fingers.*)   There's   a thought!
ARTHUR. You've never even been there.
CHARLES. I shouldn't think anybody has.
ARTHUR. *And* you'll mention "knickers" at every opportunity ... !
CHARLES. Seventh rule of comedy. "When in doubt, say 'knickers'!"
ARTHUR. I despair. (*Defeated.*) All right. We'll try it your way. Northern ... working class...

(*THEY head towards the front door.*)

CHARLES. Good!
ARTHUR. I can just imagine how you'll do it. I can just *imagine!*

(CHARLES and ARTHUR exit through the front
door.
BLACKOUT. MUSIC from radio.
LIGHTS rise on Summerskills' living room.
DORIS enters from the kitchen. SHE wears a
turban headscarf with curlers showing at the
front, a shawl, apron and clogs. SHE carries a
tray.
The crockery consists of battered tin mugs, plates,
etc. Newspaper table cloth on table. H.P.
Sauce, etc. the radio is playing a brass band
version of "Ilkley Moor B'aht tat.")

DORIS. (*Enraptured at music. Broad*
Yorkshire.) Eeee! Bah gum!

RADIO. (*Male voice. Broad Yorkshire.*)
Ayup! That were Bloody's Knicker Factory Brass
Band. A reet gradely bit o' triple tongueing there.
Now then, Radio Wigan here ... Today's Soot
Count is two tons to t'square inch ... A mite less
than yesterday. Local news ... there's trouble at
Mill again.

DORIS. Nay

RADIO. Oh, aye. A strike by t'Tripe
Manglers Union. Racing pigeon licences are
goin' up by a farthing ...

DORIS. Eeee ... that's a day's wage for a
working man!

RADIO. Ay, that it is. Now, for a bit of a
change, here's some brass band music Clagthorpe
Colliery Band.

(*Same RECORD PLAYS as before "Ilkley Moor B'aht tat ."*)

CHARLES enters from the kitchen. HE switches the RADIO OFF. HE's dressed in his idea of Northern working class clothes. A large flat cap, donkey jacket, cycle clips, clogs, etc. HE carries a dead ferret.)

CHARLES. (*Mangled Yorkshire accent.*) Ayup, mother ... t'ferret's died.

DORIS. Nay!

CHARLES. Aye ...

DORIS. Oh, well ... leave it in t'scullery. It'll do for supper.

CHARLES. (*Tosses it back into kitchen.*) Aye. (*Sits at table.*) You're a grand cook, our mother. Your cowheel and dung pie ... it's reet gradely.

(*The front DOORBELL CHIMES "Ilkley Moor B'aht tat ."*)

CHARLES. That'll be Ephraim Dullclod and his missus.

DORIS. Don't let 'em in 'til I've put in fresh curlers ... (*Exits to kitchen, taking tray.*)

CHARLES. (*Calls.*) Come in! T'doors open.

(*Enter ARTHUR and BERYL. HE wears flat cap,
donkey jacket, cycle clips, etc. SHE wears
shawl, headscarf, curlers, etc.*)

ARTHUR. (*Without enthusiasm. York-
shire.*) 'Ow do ... ayup ... bah gum ... eeee. I've
brought t'magic lantern slides.
CHARLES. Grand! (*Stands, gives Beryl a
kiss.*) Eee, Norah, you're looking reet gradely.
Let me take your shawl, you headscarf ... your
knickers.

(*ARTHUR twitches. He's obviously having some
difficulty going along with this.*)

BERYL. (*Broad Yorkshire.*) Ayeup, Jack ...
You'd turn a girl's head wi' your manly ways and
rugged good looks.
CHARLES. Aye.
ARTHUR. (*Controls himself.*) And I've
brought a jug of me homemade milk stout ...

(*A pause. CHARLES looks at him, waiting.
Normal voice.*)

ARTHUR. Oh, sorry ... (*Yorkshire.*) Ayeup!
CHARLES. Grand!

(*During above, DORIS has returned from the
kitchen, carrying a plate.*)

DORIS. Eiii ... it'll be a treat to see our 'oliday again. 'Ow do, Norah. (*Indicates plate.*) Help theeself to tripe.

ARTHUR. (*Setting up screen.*) Now, I've called t'programme, "T'Works Outing Picking Black Puddings on T'Colliery Slagheaps" ... ayeup.

BERYL. (*To Charles.*) I'll sit beside thee, you handsome bugger.

CHARLES. Aye, lass. And give us a fumble o' your grundles.

ARTHUR. (*Snaps. Normal voice.*) Just ... just a minute! "Grundles?" What the hell are "grundles?"

CHARLES. (*Normal voice.*) It's a Northern word. I made it up.

ARTHUR. You what?

CHARLES. Well, nobody knows how they actually speak ... (*Yorkshire again.*) Ayeup, mother. Pass 'round t'pigs feet butties ...

DORIS. Aye. And there'll be no talk of fumbling grundles ... not in front of Ephraim Dullclod.

ARTHUR. (*Outraged.*) "Dullclod?"

CHARLES. (*Normal.*) It's just a name! Names don't mean anything. (*To rest.*) Carry on...

BERYL. Eee, you've a smooth tongue on you, Jack Pistol.

ARTHUR. "Jack Pistol?"

(*The front DOORBELL CHIMES again, "Ilkley Moor B'aht tat ." DORIS hurries to answer it.*)

DORIS. Ayeup! That'll be t'boss. T'Gaffer! I'd know his ring anywhere. (*Opens door.*) Aye ... it's Mr. Bloody!

(*MAURICE, their literary agent, strides in. Top hat, silk, cloak, silver knobbed cane, etc. CHARLES, DORIS and BERYL tug their forelocks, curtsy, etc.*)

MAURICE. (*Yorkshire.*) Now then, lads. Production at the knicker factory is down again.
ARTHUR. (*Normal, to self.*) I don't believe this.
MAURICE. You've got to work harder. Elastic Gusset Press Operators are ten a penny.
DORIS. Come, Norah ... we'll mash tea for t'gaffer.
BERYL. Aye ...

(*The WOMEN scurry out to the kitchen taking crockery, etc., with them.*)

MAURICE. I'll not stay. I'm takin' tram to Cleethorpes. Our Tony's gettin' a silver cup ... for his winceyette bloomers.
CHARLES. Nay!
ARTHUR. Nay ... eeh, bah gum, ayeup ... (*Normal voice.*) I can't go on with this! (*Starts to

remove his cap, donkey jacket, etc.) It's ludicrous...

CHARLES. (*Yorkshire.*) What's troublin' thee, Ephraim? Is it ...?

ARTHUR. (*Normal.*) Stop it! For a start, it's all broad Yorkshire! Wigan is in Lancashire!

CHARLES. (*Normal voice.*) Is it?

ARTHUR. Of course it is!

CHARLES. Are you sure? I mean, have you been up there? Recently? Carry on ...

MAURICE. So, noses to t'grindstone, lads. Where there's muck, there's brass ...

ARTHUR. Oh, get out of here!

(*MAURICE turns and stumps out, muttering as he leaves.*)

MAURICE. Eee, bah gum ... ayeup ... there's nowt so daft as folk ... grind t'faces of t'poor ... (*Exits.*)

(*CHARLES and ARTHUR now both discard their Northern working class clothes as they talk. Toss them behind the settee, out of sight.*)

ARTHUR. I *knew* you'd do that. I knew you'd make me out to be a right idiot!

CHARLES. Ah, it's not you, Arthur. It's just a character ... based on you.

ARTHUR. And the other one based on you? (*Scorn.*) Jack Pistol! (*Simmers down.*)

(*Gradually we lose the LIGHTS on the living rooms, except for the desk area. CHARLES and ARTHUR stay within this pool of light.*)

ARTHUR. Look ... Let's try ... try ... and write it the way it happened. With normal, sensible, believable people.

CHARLES. Like Sir Arthur and Lady Persephone? "Springtime in Mayfair ..."

ARTHUR. All right! Forget that! We've got a bigger problem.

CHARLES. What?

ARTHUR. Well ... (*Sits at desk.*) ... How does it carry on? The ... the Arthur character is living with the Doris character, right? ... While his wife, the Beryl character, has moved in with the treacherous swine character. Now ...

CHARLES. I don't want to stop the flow ... but, erm ... "treacherous swine?" Um?

ARTHUR. It's not *you*. It's just a character ... based on you.

CHARLES. Go on.

ARTHUR. Now, it's not working out. I mean, I'm not ... that is ... Arthur isn't ... happy. He's missing his wife.

CHARLES. Ah. Well, the Charles ... character ... is rapidly coming to the conclusion that nookie isn't everything. I shouldn't wonder.

ARTHUR. Arthur might give him an argument there. He's put on half a stone, you know.

CHARLES. Has he? It's all that delicious food...

ARTHUR. Oh, he likes the food. There's just too much of it. It never stops.

CHARLES. Yes. You can have too much of a good thing. (*Holds his back.*)

ARTHUR. The point is, what are they going to do about the situation?

CHARLES. In episode two, you mean?

ARTHUR. What? Oh, yes.

CHARLES. Um. Tricky ... Suppose this ... this Charles fellow, who ... uh ... has perhaps not behaved as well as one might expect of a best friend ... Suppose he apologized? Um?

ARTHUR. How d'you mean?

CHARLES. Well ... he could say "I'm sorry."

ARTHUR. Go on.

CHARLES. "I've behaved like a rat" ... and ... er ...

ARTHUR. Keep going.

CHARLES. And, er ... "It'll never happen again!"

ARTHUR. (*Considers.*) No. Arthur would never accept that.

CHARLES. Oh. Are you sure? I mean, then everything could be back to square one.

ARTHUR. It'd be a damn short series. One episode.

CHARLES. Ah ...

ARTHUR. There's their wives to think of, too, y'know. It's not *entirely* the treacherous swine's fault.

CHARLES. Absolutely. Old Dullclod flew off the handle a bit sharpish.

ARTHUR. I was thinking more of Beryl ... the Beryl character. What does she see in him? He's all mouth and trousers!

CHARLES. She's not much of a catch, either! She can't cook, spends a fortune! And she's pretty sluttish around the house!

ARTHUR. (*Dangerous.*) You are talking about my wife!

CHARLES. No, I'm not.

ARTHUR. Well, it sounds like her.

CHARLES. It's *his* wife! (*Another tack.*) Who do you see playing Arthur?

ARTHUR. Oh, yes ... right. Well, erm ... it's television. I don't know if we could *get* Timothy Dalton.

CHARLES. (*Splutters with laughter, covers it.*) I think we're seeing this somewhat differently. I thought ... Ronnie Corbett.

ARTHUR. (*On dignity.*) Shall we just write it?

CHARLES. Fine. How do you see the situation developing?

ARTHUR. I don't know. Could go a number of ways.

CHARLES. For instance?

ARTHUR. Well ...

(*ARTHUR looks thoughtful. Paces into the Greys'
living room area. Bring up LIGHTS. Keep
LIGHT on desk. CHARLES watches the
action.*)

ARTHUR. ... for instance ...

(*The front door is flung open and BERYL, dressed
normally and carrying a suitcase, enters.*)

BERYL. Arthur!
ARTHUR. (*Hand to lapel, Victorian
dignity.*) Yes, Beryl?
BERYL. I've left him! Can you ever forgive
me? (*Drops on her knees, clutching at his hand.*)I
was foolish ... I was weak. I was ... a woman.
ARTHUR. You wish me to take you back?
BERYL. It's what I pray for. You're so strong,
so masculine, so noble. So different from that
weak, marshmallow of a man who led me astray.
ARTHUR. True.
DORIS. (*Hurries from the kitchen.*) Arthur!
ARTHUR. Yes, Doris?
DORIS. I've changed my mind. Take me. I'm
yours! (*SHE drops on her knees, too.*)
ARTHUR. All in good time, Doris. Carry on,
Beryl.
BERYL. I'll wash! I'll clean! I'll stop
spending money!

ARTHUR. Doris!
DORIS. I'll serve smaller portions.
BERYL. I'll learn to cook.
ARTHUR. No. Stick to what you're good at.
DORIS. I'll do all the cooking ...
BERYL. And I'll do all the ...
ARTHUR. (*Hastily.*) Yes! Yes ... Oh, very well, you can both stay.

(*THEY both stand and kiss him.*)

ARTHUR. Let's all go to bed ...

(*THEY head for the stairs. The TWO WOMEN ahead. THEY exit. ARTHUR is close behind. CHARLES stands.*)

CHARLES. Er ... Arthur!
ARTHUR. Not now, I'm busy.
CHARLES. I don't like it, Arthur.

(*ARTHUR reluctantly crosses back to the desk area. Lose LIGHTS on living rooms. Keep LIGHTS only on desk area.*)

ARTHUR. What's wrong with it?
CHARLES. It's too sophisticated.
ARTHUR. (*The wind taken out of his sail.*) Oh ... is it really? (*Smoothes hair.*)
CHARLES. And unbelievable. Two women, fancying a wimp like ...

(*Goes to point to Arthur, then points into Grey's living room.*)

CHARLES. ... him. No, no, no. It's far more likely that they'd go for ... um ... our hero.

ARTHUR. Not with his front teeth missing, they wouldn't.

CHARLES. Steady. We're looking for the same thing. But it needs laughs ... titters ... giggles ...

(*ARTHUR sits at desk, as CHARLES paces into the Summerskills' living room
LIGHTS up on living room.*)

ARTHUR. (*Sarcastic.*) Really?

CHARLES. It needs *pace.* Perhaps even a touch of ... *farce!* (*His trousers drop around his ankles.*)

(*BERYL rushes in from the kitchen. SHE wears bra, panties, suspender belt, etc.*)

BERYL. Charles! My husband's found out about us! He's on his way over!

CHARLES. Quick! Hide under the lampshade!

(*SHE plucks the large lampshade off its stand, puts it over her head and stands to attention as*

*... MISS TROTTER enters through the front
door. SHE's wearing a full nun's habit. SHE
reacts to Charles' bare legs.)*

MISS TROTTER. Ooooh!
CHARLES. (*Quickly pulling up trousers.*)
I'm sorry, Sister. It's my trousers. They fall down
every time I tell a lie. The doctors are baffled.
MISS TROTTER. (*Throws back her cowl.*)
No, no, I'm not a nun, Charles!
CHARLES. Miss Lushbody! Fifi ...!
MISS TROTTER. My husband's found out
about us! He's on his way over!
CHARLES. Quick! Hide behind the screen!

(*SHE plucks some flowers from a vase. Dashes
the water over her chest.*)

MISS TROTTER. Yes. Oh, dear! Now I'll
have to take it off!
CHARLES. Yes, yes, yes ... (*He pushes her
behind the screen.*)

(*During the following, SHE tosses the bits and
pieces of the nun's habit over the top of the
screen. SHE's getting undressed. The RADIO
CLICKS on, without being touched. CHARLES
reacts to it.*)

RADIO. (*Male voice.*) Here is a news flash! An escaped lunatic is in your area, disguised as an Arab.

CHARLES. What?

RADIO. An *Arab.* That is the end of the news flash. (*CLICKS OFF.*)

(*The W.C. door bursts open and DORIS rushes in, in bra, panties and suspender belt.*)

DORIS. Charles! My husband's found out about us! He's on his way over!

CHARLES. Quick! Hide behind the ... (*Take.*) Just a minute ... *I'm* your husband!

DORIS. That's no reason to take risks!

CHARLES. That's true. Quick! Behind the settee!

(*SHE ducks down behind the settee as ... the front door bursts open and MAURICE enters, dressed in full Arab costume, complete with sword.*)

MAURICE. (*Arab accent.*) So ... Infidel! I hear you are having an affair with several of my wives!

CHARLES. It's not true! (*His trousers fall down.*)

(*The THREE LADIES appear from their hiding places, one after the other. MISS TROTTER, is now also down to bra, panties, and suspender belt.)*

BERYL. Abdul?!
DORIS. Abdul?!
MISS TROTTER. Abdul?!
MAURICE. To the harem!

(HE sweeps all THREE WOMEN out of the front door. SQUEALS of delight.
ARTHUR who has been watching this from the desk area, stands.)

ARTHUR. Hold it! Who the f ... who is Abdul?!

(CHARLES pulls up his trousers, crosses to the desk area. Lose LIGHTS on living rooms. Only the desk area is LIT.)

CHARLES. The comic Arab. Tenth rule of comedy.
ARTHUR. And the nun?
CHARLES. Eleventh.
ARTHUR. Hah! Is that the height of your ambition? To write a cheap, vulgar farce?
CHARLES. Of *course* it isn't! *(HE clutches the waistband of his trousers.)*
ARTHUR. Nuns! Arabs! Trousers falling down every time you tell a lie! It's ridiculous. No,

what we need is a believable twist ... A surprise development.

(*HE puts his arm around Charles. THEY move into the Greys' living room, as it LIGHTS UP.*)

CHARLES. Ye-ess ...
ARTHUR. Let's say we ... we find the two men arguing.
CHARLES. It would make a change, I suppose.
ARTHUR. And suddenly, there's a knock at the front door ...

(*The DOORBELL RINGS.*)

ARTHUR. ... or possible a ring.

(*Enter MISS TROTTER, now dressed. SHE carries a handbag. ARTHUR moves back to the desk and watches.*)

MISS TROTTER. Cooee! It's only me.
CHARLES. Ah, Miss Trotter.
MISS TROTTER. No, please ... Maude. (*Exposes a bare shoulder.*)
CHARLES. M-Maude?
MISS TROTTER. For too long I've concealed my passion for you, Charles.

(*ARTHUR sits at the desk, beaming his approval of the scene.*)

MISS TROTTER. Take me! Take me in your manly arms and crush me to your bosom!

CHARLES. Oh ... my ... God ...

MISS TROTTER. My heart beats for you and you alone ... (*SHE paws him lasciviously, pulling him down onto the settee.*) ... my wild, tempestuous gypsy!

CHARLES. (*To Arthur.*) Get her off me! (*To Miss Trotter.*) Please, madam! Not today, thank you ...

MISS TROTTER. I see. (*SHE gets off him. THEY stand.*) Spurned! Very well ... if I cannot have you, none other shall!

(*SHE pulls a gun from her handbag and shoots him at point blank range.*
BANG! Astonished, CHARLES falls backwards over the settee and disappears behind it. MISS TROTTER heads for the front door. Pauses.)

MISS TROTTER. (*Mainly to self.*) Fancy that! A murder in our street! I must tell all the neighbors! (*Blows the smoke from her gun and exits.*)

ARTHUR. (*Applauds from the desk.*) Like it! Like it!

CHARLES. (*Looking a little frazzled, clambers into view over the back of the settee.*) A ... b-believable twist?!

ARTHUR. (*Smug.*) I believed it.

CHARLES. You've cracked! (*HE joins him at the desk.*) You've gone off your trolley! 'Round the bend! (*Picks up a paper knife. Advances on ARTHUR, who backs away around the desk.*) Come here!

(*During the following, ARTHUR steps up onto a desk chair, and from there onto the desk, trying to get away from Charles.*)

ARTHUR. Take it easy, Charles ... I just thought, with you dead, it'd be easier to sort out the ... have a happy ending and ... maybe not ...

CHARLES. It isn't working, this wife swapping idea. It's too close to home.

ARTHUR. All right ... let's forget it. Start afresh ... truce ?

CHARLES. (*Reluctantly.*) Truce. (*HE sits at desk. Puts his head in his hands.*)

ARTHUR. Give me a title ...

CHARLES. Um ...

(*Slowly bring up LIGHTS on both living rooms. Hold the position, which is identical to that At Rise.*

ARTHUR standing on desk, deep in thought. CHARLES sitting, head in hands, also deep in thought. NOISES "er," "um," etc. as before.)

CHARLES. "I ... Married ... A ... Mermaid!"
ARTHUR. Is it different enough?
CHARLES. No ... let's think of another title...

(The kitchen door opens and DORIS enters. SHE wears a flowered pinafore.)

DORIS. Next door's cat's done a whoopsie in the bird bath.

(ARTHUR and CHARLES look at each other hopefully.)

CHARLES. No, it's too long.
DORIS. *(To Charles.)* Dinner in twenty minutes, dear. *(To Arthur.)* Are you staying, Arthur?
ARTHUR. No, no. Beryl will be cooking mine ... I'm afraid. *(Gathering his notes together, has a thought, prompted by the notes.)*

(DORIS exits to the kitchen.)

ARTHUR. I still think there's something in two situation comedy writers ... they swap wives ... but they have to go on working together.

CHARLES. We just tried that! We couldn't agree on an ending.

ARTHUR. (*Rueful.*) No.

CHARLES. Besides, I'm not sure it's right for television. (*A thought.*) I'll tell you what, though...

ARTHUR. What?

CHARLES. It might make a stage play.

ARTHUR. (*Intrigued.*) How would you end it?

CHARLES. Simple. (*Takes pen and writes on notes.*) You just write ... "Curtain!"

ARTHUR. Isn't that a bit of a cop-out?

CHARLES. Of course it's not.

ARTHUR. You're absolutely right. It isn't!

(*Both their trousers fall down.*)

ARTHUR and CHARLES. Oooops!

CURTAIN

PROPERTY LIST

Pre-set

1 tin of stew in saucepan on stove with wooden spoon. (Start heating through on the 15-minute call.)

4 measures of Smash in mixing bowl. (Done in interval.)

Pre-cook 2 sausages and 2 slices of toast.

Pre-set 2 sausage and 2 slices of toast and false food on a spare plate.

Make flask of coffee.

Refill kettle (this is for Smash and coffee during the interval)

Pre-set brown tray with blue patterned plate and piece of cellophane.

Put 2 spoonfuls of rice pudding in speckled bowl.

Put opened packet of crisps in 1 octagonal bowl.

From packet of crisps take 2 and break them up into other octagonal bowl.

On-stage Pre-set

1) Swap drinks tray and radio, put *TV Times* picture in front of radio. 4 whisky tumblers on drinks tray and fresh bottle of Bell's Whisky on drinks shelf. Stand records up an sway dead ivy and parlor palm and fern for live ones.

2) Fold screen up and lean on P.S. wall U.S. of serving hatch.

3) Set live looking flowers on P.S. dining table on doily and mat, making sure there is enough water in the vase of live flowers.

4) Strike clothes from under P.S. sofa and P.S. armchair cushions along with kimono from desk drawer and put in U.S.P.S. quick change area.

5) Plump cushions on P.S. sofa and armchair and set "Arthur's" jacket on back of P.S. sofa.

6) Reset enamel jug and lantern with ferret U.S.P.S.

7) Strike rubber gloves, dusters and polish from desk drawer and reset in P.S. kitchen (Off stage.)

8) Place 1 sheet of typed paper in typewriter.

9) Reset wicker stool D.S. of desk on marks.

10) Remove small cup, Alka-Seltzer, sun cream, coke can and orange juice box from white bin and place on D.S.C. coffee table along with white mug from P.S. dining table and 1 packet of silk cut and lighter from P.S. prop table. Place 1/2 bottle of Grant's whisky on D.S.C. coffee table.

11) Empty contents of white bin into Grey's blue bin removing cigarette butts to refill glass ashtray on D.S.C. coffee table.

12) Place dressing underneath D.S.C. coffee table onto Grey's side.

13) Set Espane bag, camera box, plastic bag and white box O.P. side of desk. Remove rubbish

from U.S.P.S. wicker basket and place in white box. Remove magazines and newspapers from filing cabinet and drinks cabinet and place on floor U.S.O.P. of desk.

14) Remove small table from stairwell U.S.O.P. and place with nest of tables C.P. of chesterfield sofa.

15) Swap dressing from underneath P.S. nest of tables to underneath O.P. nest of tables.

16) Strike magazines from P.S. nest of tables and P.S. sofa, along with nail file to P.S. props table.

17) Set dressing around record case and piano stool and Bible.

18) Open piano, reset sheet music, glass vase and 4 wine glasses. Tilt picture above piano to a crooked position.

19) Set red squeegy mop and tub U.S. of kitchen door on O.P.

20) Shove blanket, Christmas tree, roll of wallpaper into stairwell with T-chest and place ironing board in front. Along with projector screen, projector,carousels and cardboard box with dustpan on top. Set stairs dressing.

21) Set cardboard box lid, wood, cricket bat, golf club, umbrella, curtain tracks in U.S.O.P. hallway.

22) Hang coats on hangers from wall light practical on coat stand U.S.P.S. hallway.

23) Reset dressing D.S.C. to underneath stool D.S.C. along with box file and coffee pot.

24) Place 1 sheet of typed paper (slightly crumpled) and 1 sheet of very thin white paper (from desk drawer) with black writing on it in white bin D.S. of desk.

25) Straighten lamp shade U.S. of desk.

26) Put fullers earth on O.P. dining table with magazine. Fullers earth O.P. nest of tables with leaflets and small glass ashtray.

28) Make sure O.P. cellar and bathroom doors are shut.

Offstage P.S. (Summerskill's)

Door slam (U.S.P.S. in hallway)

P.S. Prop table

Tea towel and cutlery (2 knives/2 forks)
2 plates (cream colored)
4 large plain wine glasses
Bowl and packet of crisps (opened)
Pie dish and oven gloves
Pile of bills
Pile of Magazines (2)
Nail file
White clutch bag (Beryl's)
Bowl of cold rice pudding and spoon
Cabbage

On Floor, left of P.S. Prop Table

Maurice's briefcase
Small red suitcase
Pink blanket

On Floor, right of P.S. Prop Table

Enamel jug
Ferret
Magic lantern

Offstage P.S. (In Summerskill's kitchen)

Rummage box (tea-chest)
2 cardboard boxes with pot and pans
2 piles of "recipe" books ties with string
Pile consisting of : roasting tin: quiche tin,
frying pan

On Floor, D.S. of Rostrum

Vacuum cleaner (working)
Spray polish
Duster
Rubber gloves
Talcum powder (to dust Trevor's hand)

On Speaker Inside Kitchen

Tin tray with the following on it:
Enamel Plate
Pork Pie (on enamel plate)
Knife/Fork
Enamel mug
H.P. Sauce
Plate of tripe

On Floor next to Speaker

Slops bucket

Against U.S.P.S. Hallway Wall (Offstage side)

Cap and hose of hood hairdryer
Large red suitcase
Red vanity case

By U.S.P. S> Quick Change Area

Pile of Beryl's clothes on hangers (strung together)
   1 pink satin dress
   1 rainbow sun dress

On Midstage P.S. Quick Change Table

Cigarette holder and cigarette

Offstage O.P. (Grey's)

Door slam (in Hallway)

On Prop Table in Kitchen

Knife and fork
Bag of sugar (to put in cup)
Brown tray with plate of lumpy stew and piece
of cellophane
Nutmeg
Flask of coffee
2 cups and saucers
2 Brown casserole dishes (1 with casserole in)
5 place mats
2 dinner plates
2 knives and forks
2 serving spoons
Salt & Pepper pots
Candelabra
Covered silver salver with the following on it:
    Silver tea pot
    Silver leaf tray containing bread and
butter, caviar, quails, H.P. sauce, vase of flowers

On U.S.O.P. Prop Table

Daily Express Newspaper
Plasticine truffles (to put in cup)
Comb
Tea cup (for sugar)
Tea cup (for truffles)
1 bottle of sultana wine
Coffee cup and saucer
Blouse
Tights
Petticoat
Teddy (all-in-one underwear)
Cami-knickers
Half slip
Travel rug

Wine Cellar

Cardboard box containing:
    3 bottles of pea wine
    1 bottle of radish wine
    4 other bottles of wine
    2 bottles of "expensive wine" (set on floor)

U.S.O.P. Quick Change Area

Sword (with Mr. Morris' Arab costume)
Silver-Topped cane (with Mr. Morris'
Victorian costume)

U.S.C. Quick Change Area

Brown handbag containing starting pistol
N.B. Chamber must be fully loaded with
blanks. After each performance unload gun and
lock away. Oil gun regularly. Never dry fire.